MORE I COULD NOT ASK

More I Could Not Ask

JAMES PETERSON

A Crossroad Book
The Crossroad Publishing Company
New York

The Crossroad Publishing Company
370 Lexington Avenue, New York, NY 10017

Printed in the United States of America

Library of Congress Catalog Card Number: 98-74688

ISBN: 0-8245-1772-5

1   2   3   4   5   6   7   8   9   10   03   02   01   00   99

To
Jesus Christ
Savior, Lord, Giver of the Spirit,
who came
to bring freedom to us all,
and to Mary,
who never ceases to be Mother
to the imprisoned people of the earth—
all of us

Contents

Acknowledgments

WHAT I HAVE WRITTEN HERE IS NOT A HISTORY BUT AN ACT OF thanksgiving to God. It describes an interior journey that has been guided by his grace through the changing world of the twentieth century.

I write also to thank the people who have shared my life and made possible the joy of living and giving and growing. They are too numerous to mention and many are too individually beautiful to describe. Some I will know well again only in the Communion of Saints.

In a special way I am indebted to those who have assisted in bringing this work into its present state. Most especially Pat O'Connor has contributed generously in reworking the manuscript; likewise Woody Foster for his helpful reading and commentaries. Pat Owens, Sister Gertrude Marie, Sister Lisa Mary, Bernie Kerner, and Lynn Quinn have cared and shared enough to give existence to my hopes.

For anyone who takes time to read and reflect, I am most grateful. You help to fulfill my life.

Part One

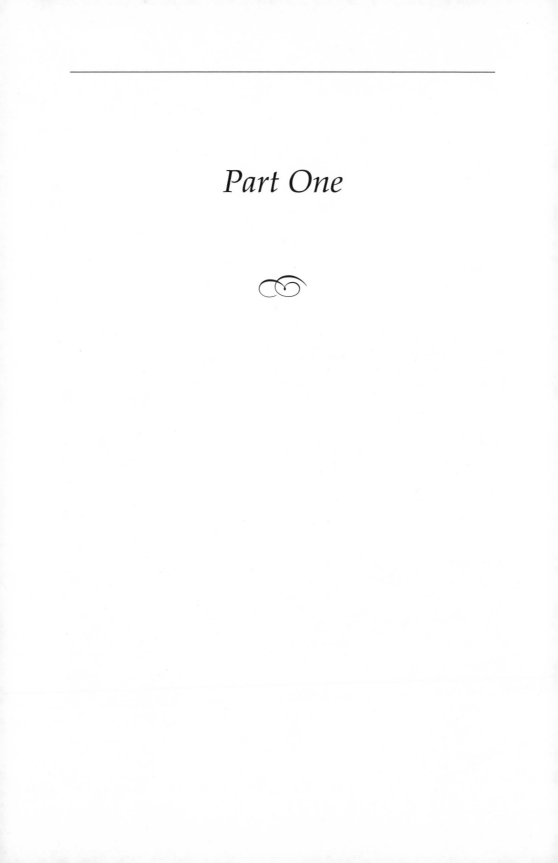

1

Pine Avenue

I WAS SITTING WITH MY EYES CLOSED IN THE MIDDLE OF A GROUP of ex-convicts, alcoholics, drug addicts, and street people. A young deacon who had come at my invitation to give us some guidance into prayer was leading us in a meditation. Although I was much at ease with the men, when the deacon asked us to let our imaginations run free, I was uncomfortable. For years the imagination had not been of any real help to me in prayer; it was a distraction. Yet I tried to follow as he was leading-us-in-darkness. He asked us to imagine that we were sitting on a hillside overlooking the city of Erie. We were to take some time and consider what we saw.

That wasn't difficult. For years I had lived as spiritual director at St. Mark's seminary. The city of Erie lay down below it in surprising clarity. The steeples of the various Catholic parishes were landmarks. There was the Cathedral where I had been ordained; there was St. John's where I had grown up, had gone to grade school, and had said my first Mass. That was my childhood home. The house was still there but I didn't know who lived in it. Beyond the city were the bay, the peninsula, Lake Erie, and the firmament.

Then the deacon told us mentally to come down from the hill, go into the city, and look for some place where we could meet God. I "got up," half expecting to go to St. Peter's Cathedral, a marvelous monument to faith. Without deciding to, I went instead to St. Patrick's Haven, an overnight shelter for homeless men. St. Patrick's has no rules except against violence and theft. Many who are barred from other shelters for violating rules come to St. Patrick's as the only alternative to sleeping in cars or doorways or walking the streets. It was there that I went to find God.

That came as a complete surprise to me. As a child, I had felt safe with the members of my family. Mom and Dad, Ward and Marie and Jack and Bob and Tom were part of a world that was always secure and nurturing. Together we lived—and prayed, especially in moments of stress. When I left Pine Avenue to go to high school, to camp, or for a vacation, I always had the sense of being on an adventure with a place to come back to.

As a seminarian, I had felt the passing of that home as I came to a life of joy in the presence of Christ, the love of Mary, and the communion of saints. As time went on, it seemed that going back to Pine Avenue was an adventure. Just before I was ordained I dreaded the notion of going into active ministry. I had come to love quiet and prayer; silence wasn't the slightest threat. The world held no excitement that could challenge recollection.

Even after I was ordained, I wanted, needed, and found strength in hours of prayer every day. The Mass, the Eucharist, supplied the nourishment I needed for the further journey. But here, in undirected prayer, I walked right past the home of my childhood, the homes of my brothers and sister, the college and institutions where I had taught for many years, the churches where I had celebrated liturgy and been caught up in silent prayer. In my meditation I walked instead into the city where I had lived most of my life, teeming with the monuments of my major memories.

I walked straight to St. Patrick's Haven. A number of the men there were certainly mental cases; several were under the influence of alcohol or drugs, though not enough to be disruptive. They accepted me easily,

"Father Pete, will you be in your office tomorrow?"

"Is Tom still at your place? How's he doing?"

"I might come there if you have room."

We'd drift off into one-on-one sessions. On rare occasions the session would involve confession, but often it would involve praying together.

And no strain. I knew I would much prefer spending a day in jail to most of the forms of recreation that might seem an alternative. To help with a mission at the state penitentiary at Rockview is immensely more attractive to me than a free pass to the Superbowl, or a concert, or an opera.

For years I was the youngest priest at any gathering of clergy, the youngest teacher at Gannon College. Eventually I was one of the oldest. But I always had trouble relating to people as older or younger. That meant no more to me than color, financial state, sex, or religion. It was important to come together person to person. The sharing that took place then was not based on a formula or a prearranged plan. It was just an encounter where there could be a free flow to the extent that there was trust.

Somehow over the years I have had a gift that makes it easy for people to trust. And somehow with the most broken, the trust makes possible a richer exchange. When we're together in Christ's name, he is with us. With convicts, with addicts, with the consciously broken, it's easier to be together. But we are also more together, and Christ is more fully in the midst of us. Sometimes I wonder how that came about. I know it is a work of God's providence, but he works through the events of our lives. Some people assume that I am an addict or a recovering alcoholic. They say, "In order to help, you have to have been through it."

If I were to outguess God in his providence, I'd look for someone for prison ministry among those who had been brutalized by a dysfunctional society and then made a turnaround. In finding a new direction, he or she would still be mindful of the others who were still suffering. Then, without getting lost in pursuit of the fringe benefits I have missed, the renewed person would have an understanding of those still trapped, a strength that came from God and a commitment to the service of others. In Alcoholics Anonymous (AA) that's called the twelfth step.

But that was not what happened with me. The world in which I grew up was tremendously protected and loving. My world had a my-father-is-bigger-than-your-father security. Mom and Dad had the happiest marriage I ever knew—and the earliest thought I can remember is that my mother really wanted me to be happy. I assumed that all people were surrounded by such love.

We were poor. Mom was orphaned when she was eleven; Dad's father left when Dad was only in the third grade. The only one of our grandparents we ever met was Dad's mother. Gramma was a thin woman. When I think of her, I remember wrinkles upon wrinkles. She wore long dresses, usually brown or black, and high leather shoes with low heels and buttons. I have two vivid memories of her.

Once she was taking care of us when Mom was in the hospital having another baby. I went out into the back yard and wandered into our chicken coop. We had raised the chickens from chicks, and they were just maturing. We had built nests, but the chickens weren't using them yet. Then I looked into a nest and there was a splendid white egg. I couldn't believe it. I touched it to be sure it wasn't a glass decoy. When I had determined that it was real, I went running into the house and grabbed Gramma's long apron,

"Gramma, come quick!"

Startled, she asked, "What is it?"

"I can't tell you. You've got to come."

We hurried out of the house and into the chicken coop. I led her to the nest and majestically pointed to the egg. Realizing that my wonder was over a simple egg, she bent down, lifted me up, and hugged me—and she was not a hugging person—then she just laughed and laughed.

I also remember when she died. We were too young to go to the funeral, but someone took us for just a short time to her home, where she was laid out. When we came, Dad was crying. That surprised me. I went over and stared at Gramma in the casket. Her hair was beautiful; her face was not quite so lined. She had on a lavender dress, not brown or black—nothing you could really work in. There was a little cloth over her feet. When I lifted it up, she had on red watered-silk shoes with high heels. I dropped the cloth in a hurry and wanted to leave. I don't remember asking anyone all the questions that were on my mind.

My grandmother's parents, Cornelius and Margaret O'Neill, had been born in Ireland. Cornelius had been a schoolteacher, but when famine struck his family hard, he and Margaret went to Liverpool, where my grandmother was born. She never acknowledged that she had been born in England. That was a scar which, like her age, she felt she had a right to conceal.

Her parents settled in Union City, Pennsylvania, in the second half of the nineteenth century. It was there, in the rectory of St. Teresa's Church, that she married William Peterson, who was not a Catholic. In rapid succession, they had three children: Cornelius (my father), Margaret, and Cassie. Then they broke up. What I learned through my aunts was that their father started running with other women. They were poor and Gramma had nothing to fall back on, but she would not dream of raising her children with such an example in the house. Years later I learned that when they were hardly able to provide for their three children, Gramma refused to have more. And since she would not think of avoiding children by any means other than refusing to have sex, he started to run with other women.

Eventually, she walked into Union City with her children and only the clothes they could wear and carry. She began to make a living by doing laundry for fifty cents a day. Life for her and the children was hard. They would walk along railroad tracks and pick up coal that had fallen off the passing trains. Often in winter they would have to break the ice on their water basin so they could wash before going to school.

Dad had a dog named Jim (his favorite dog, for whom I was reputedly named!) who sometimes was fast enough to catch a rabbit. I was never sure if that was a remarkable dog or a remarkable story, but I knew that wild game was one of their best sources for meat.

Dad dropped out of school and went to work on a farm out in the country. On Saturdays he would walk to town with his pay of fifty cents to give to his mother to help out. He got bigger and stronger, and when he could not find work in Union City, he went west and found work in a lumber camp in Oregon. We had pictures of him as part of a basketball team. He was wiry and handsome, a bit wild, and lonesome. When he came back east, unannounced and unexpected, Gramma, without batting an eye, without an exclamation or a hug, simply asked "Con, would you like a cup of tea?" He would!

He found work. And he found Mom, Gertrude Ward, an orphan.

He was a big man, a bit rough, self-made, six feet tall, with a fine mind but little education. Mom was a little woman, much closer to five feet than six, with hair that came down to her waist. Years later Dad told me he thought that if he had not met Mom, he would have become a bum. I thought he was kidding, until some years later when I moved to Union City and met young men everywhere who could not get any steady work, with girls who were available and lonesome. They had little family life behind them and little family life ahead of them.

We have wedding pictures that are still beautiful—black and white, fading, but full of joy and truth. Dad borrowed money from Mom's sister Minnie so he could take Mom on a honeymoon at Geneva-On-The-Lake, Ohio. That was her first experience of travel. Things and scenery were never as important to her as people.

Home was the center of our lives. On Saturday nights, we would pester Dad and Mom to make shadows for us to guess. They'd put up a sheet in the bathroom doorway and with their fingers produce the outline of a fox's head, a dog running, a water pail. When we got our first radio, the kids weren't allowed to turn it on. We knew the schedule well, and we'd sit quietly for *Amos and Andy,* the *Lux Radio Theater,* the *Hit Parade,* the *March of Time* (where each week death came to somebody else). When the heavyweight fights were on, we'd be in bed, half asleep, and Dad would open the sliding door to the boys' room and say, "Fight's over. Louis won."

The highway that went past our house had some fast-moving traffic. Sooner or later every dog we had was killed by a passing car. All of us children—three, four, five, or six (however many we had at the time)— would be crushed and broken by the loss of a family member. At supper, while we were still in mourning, Dad would say, "That settles it! No more dogs. They're too much trouble." We would not protest: even when I was very young, it seemed to me impossible to solve the loss of a dog by getting some stranger to replace it. But after some time, when the hurt was mostly gone, we would hear of a dog that needed a home. We'd go to Mom and start to campaign. She'd get Dad to change his mind, and we'd have a dog again.

We never had any questions about whether Mom and Dad loved us. Except for their very strong and simple Catholic faith and their love for each other, we were the center of their lives. Dad's greatest gift to us was Mom. She was gentle, simple, and trusting. She was always there. Once I heard him tell Mom to shut up. I could hardly believe it! No one ever talked to her like that. If one of us got mouthy and Dad heard it, his big voice would fill the whole house: "Jim, don't let me ever hear you talk to your mother like that. She takes care of us all the time and I'm not going to let any snip like you make her life harder." And that was that. But now Dad came right out and said, "Shut up!" He was looking for a hammer, going through one of the several catch-all drawers we had around the house. Mom said she had told him to put the hammer up high, because the kids would never let it alone if they could get hold of it, but he didn't listen to her. He yelled "Shut up!" and the silence was deafening. Mom didn't say a word. A few minutes later he apologized and it was all over.

In our home there were only three bedrooms: one for Mom and Dad, one for boys, and one for Marie, the only girl. Newly born infants could share a room with her, but eventually each new boy would come into our bedroom, where in the end the five of us slept in wall-to-wall beds and cots. If any of us would complain of the injustice, Marie would be quick to point out that the work was divided the same way as the bedrooms. She did half.

On Christmas Eve, Mom would light a little red vigil light and put it in our back window, which looked out over far-reaching fields. That was in case any strangers were lost out there; they'd see the light and be able to find their way and we'd take care of them. I thought that was wonderful, though I never thought to worry about what a lost person would do the other 364 days of the year. I'd stand there and look out so I could call Dad if I saw anybody. The first few years we went to bed without seeing the tree. Later we could stay up till it was decorated. With morning came the surprises! Presents from Santa Claus! We'd pass over the pants or long underwear from Dad's sisters Cassie and Margaret to get to the important things—some toys, or an axe, or a bottle of olives. Cassie and Minnie were always part of celebrating, part of that world where we knew everyone loved us.

At church, the men and boys went to one side, the women and girls to the other. The altars were magnificent in red and gold. Father Heibel, having read the Gospel in Latin at the altar, would read it again from the tall wooden pulpit, this time in English: "A decree went forth from Caesar Augustus that the whole world should be enrolled and Joseph and Mary would go to Bethlehem, because he was of the family of David." And the shepherds—and we with them—would leave the sheep and other things to find a child wrapped in swaddling clothes and lying in a manger.

The choir would sing Latin hymns that had too great a range for their voices—but the organ covered over a lot. Then it would get very quiet, and Marie Zimmerman, the organist who seemed as old as the church, would play the Largo from *Xerxes* and sound the chimes. Finally, we'd all sing "Holy God, We Praise Thy Name." And I didn't even care that Father Heibel was singing loud and off-key, I just knew that my voice meant as much as anybody else's, and our voices touched each other and lifted each other. From year to year I looked forward to that final "Holy God" as the best singing we did at St. John's. I don't mean art, but love and sharing.

Later in the day we'd drive down to Aunt Cassie's or Aunt Margaret's and *really* eat—ham, cake, ice cream, and pumpkin or apple pie. We'd go over to Aunt Minnie's, whose house was still lighted with gas lamps. On the way home we'd drive to Perry Square to see the fountain of water lit up with different colored lights. We'd drive through Glenwood to see all the lights the rich people had on their houses to celebrate Christmas. Then we'd go home. When we had to go to bed, we'd ask Dad and Mom to leave the Christmas tree lights on and leave our bedroom door open. Each of the five of us boys sharing a bedroom would kneel down separately and say our prayers. We'd crawl into bed and have to be quiet because the door was open. Soon I'd hear one breathing the steady breath of sleep. Then another. I didn't really want to go to sleep. There was so much to think about. But I just couldn't stay awake, not even with the door open and the Christmas tree lights on.

Dad was a combination millhand and salesman at a lumber company. He was an honest man, and people trusted him. I can remember that he always had to wear a truss because he had a hernia, and we couldn't afford the operation he needed. Mom and Dad never bought much for themselves. She'd wear a winter coat for years. He'd want her to get a new one, but she'd want him to get a suit to look more like a salesman. With six kids to support, he couldn't demand much at work—he needed the job too much.

Our house was almost at the edge of town. There was room for a garden, for rabbits, and for chickens. Sometimes we'd watch Dad kill the chickens. He'd cut off their heads with an axe, dip them into real hot water and pluck their feathers, and singe the hair off their skin over the gas flames. We would eat the chickens if we didn't know which one we were eating. If we knew the chicken personally, we didn't want anything to do with it.

The yard had three beaten-up garages and a natural gas well. It didn't provide enough gas for heating, but it was enough for cooking and for turning every pan in the house completely black. We lived downstairs in the two-story house and had tenants in the upstairs and in a bungalow on the same lot. In our yard we had pear, peach, apple, and cherry trees, a small row of grapevines, rhubarb, dahlias, gladiolus, zinnias, nasturtiums, tomatoes, beans, carrots, and a mixture of weeds.

The day I started school I cried. Mom took me into the first grade. There were thirty-six double seats. By the time class started, they were all filled. Mom brought me to a seat that was already half taken and said, "Here's a nice boy—you can be friends." He was bigger than I was, and it wasn't very long till I found out he had flunked first grade the year before and had to take it again. Nobody liked him, including me.

We lived in St. John's parish, an old German parish with a powerful tradition, a pastor both stern and genuine, and a Sister of St. Joseph for every classroom. Sister Rose Irma was a very little woman, but the seventy-two of us really knew who was in charge. I was afraid of her from the start. The whole business scared me. We all had to go to the restrooms in the basement at the same time. If we really needed to go, we could raise our hands and ask for permission, but Sister didn't like it. Once I wet my pants and tried to pretend that nothing happened. No one ever noticed, or at least no one ever said anything. But I knew I was a coward. I felt I was in over my head, but I would never tell Mom or Dad because they'd be disappointed.

The great outdoors was a joy. Being out in the open grew on all of us.

I suppose this appreciation was partly because our house was crowded, but the outdoors were an invitation in themselves. As a Boy Scout I'd go on hikes, sometimes overnight, even in winter. Every summer we'd go to Lake Erie or French Creek for a week's camping, a bargain at $4.00. We couldn't afford an established camp, so Dad and the other men would do most of the work. We used hand-dug latrines and homemade everything. When we were a bit older, we could hike out into the country with a lunch, passing the day swimming, climbing the hills, lying under the trees.

A few times each year we'd go out to Union City to Uncle Con's dairy farm. His dog, Shep, was *the* dog of my childhood. He would go out into the cow pasture and bring in the cows for milking. He wouldn't let the bull or the heifers or even the cows that were dried up get near the barn. How he knew which were which I don't know, but he could handle that whole herd. When he finished his work, he'd play with us again as though he had done nothing. French Creek ran through the pasture, clear and rippling. Once I went fishing. I caught one, but it seemed too small to keep, so I threw it back. It swam away so happily that I never went fishing again.

The same thing happened with hunting. Dad had a license every year. Many a Saturday he'd come home with four rabbits. Ward got to be a good shot too. When we finally had enough guns, I went too. I saw a little gray squirrel running happily from branch to branch. He wasn't hurting me at all, so I shot over his head and gave up hunting.

But I never gave up the woods, or hiking, or listening to the water, especially the waves. I enjoyed Lake Pleasant, but sometimes we'd go to the peninsula and the waves on Lake Erie would come in endlessly. The gravel would go in and out... in and out.

Sometimes, we'd go to the Pine Woods, where Dad was born. The foundation of his family's house was still there. Aunt Cassie would roll down the hill with us. When we were worn out with laughing, she'd tell us to be still and listen. There was always something new. Two or three times a summer, we'd go out into the country to pick blackberries. Dad could go through briars easily, but I'd get all torn apart. He could do it even quietly. I guess it's something you have to learn for rabbit hunting. We'd get elderberries too, just growing along the road. Mom would can those too, mainly for pies.

Once when I was wandering through the fields behind our house—the very fields from which anyone who was lost could see our red vigil light on Christmas Eve—I looked up and the sun was orange. In large, old-English-style letters I read *IHS* as clear as could be. It was like a huge host out there in the fields to guide anyone who was wandering. I didn't say anything to anyone, except one of my brothers. He said it was probably telephone wires, but there weren't any telephone wires there. No telephone poles. Just me, wandering.

∽

In 1929, the Depression hit hard, and Dad lost his job. Luckily, though, Ward had a paper route, and for some time, except for the rent from the tenants, the only family income was from Ward's paper route. We were behind in payments to the Building and Loan, and we couldn't get caught up on our payments at Ebert's grocery store. Sometimes Mr. Ebert would holler at us, asking for the money, and Dad would get mad, but we just didn't have it. When I look back, I wonder at Dad's humility in eating with money that came from one of the kid's paper routes.

Sometimes Dad would call up and say he'd found strawberries cheap. Marie would bake biscuits and we'd have strawberry shortcake like millionaires. Any summer day Dad wanted, he'd call Mom and say, "Let's go out to Lake Pleasant." No matter what she was cooking, she'd say yes, and we'd drive out to the lake and have a picnic and just let the cool evening sink in and comfort us.

There was such love and peace in our home, but a few times that serenity was threatened. Before my youngest brother, Tom, was born, Mom had to stay in bed for weeks. She was in her forties, and she had lost one child before it was born. Even though it was the Christmas season, the doctor said she couldn't be active at all. Dad called us together in a meeting and told us he really needed us. We'd have to take care of the house and get it ready for Christmas, and see that Jack and Bob were all right. There'd be no fighting, because that would be hard on Mom. And we really needed to pray. Ward was worried, and when he told Sister at school, she lit a candle and the whole class prayed for Mom. The candle was there to remind them to keep praying.

Father Heibel used to walk up to our house almost every day. I was amazed at this, because he always seemed so stern at school. But when Mom was sick, he'd walk onto the porch and with a very soft voice, almost falsetto, he'd ask if she were awake. He'd talk, they'd pray, and she always felt better, more hopeful, when he left.

Christmas came and went and it was beautiful. On January 18, Tom arrived, and after a while we knew Mom was going to be all right. Dad could smile again, and once in a while we could even have a good fight.

When Tom was ten years old, Mom got very sick again. Her gall bladder had been causing her trouble. Her sister, Ida, had died of cancer, so she was worried. In the hospital, after surgery, complications developed and jaundice set in. She was anointed again. At that time anointing was usually linked to danger of death. I was about fifteen, so I could get into the hospital to see her. She told me what she wanted at her funeral because she knew she just couldn't talk to Dad about it. She didn't want a big splash, no expensive casket, no boy scouts, no flags, and nothing that would make more pressure for Dad.

When she finished, I told her I'd take care of it if I had to, but I also told her that I didn't think she was trying hard enough to get well. She looked at me in complete amazement. Then she said, no, she wasn't really trying. She explained that ten years before, when Tom had been born and they didn't think she was going to live, she had asked God if she could have just ten years to get Tom started. Somehow she felt that if you carry a child yourself, you can understand him better; that no matter how hard a stranger tries, she just can't take care of someone else's child quite as well. So she told God that if she could have just those ten years, she wouldn't ask him for anything else. Tom was now ten and it wouldn't be right to try.

I wasn't a theologian, but it didn't sound right to me, so I said, "Mom, that doesn't mean you shouldn't try. Maybe God just wants you to love us enough to try harder—not for you, but for Tom and Bob and Jack and all of us. Just tell him you're going to do your best to get well, and if that isn't what he wants, you're willing that he should take you. That's not asking for anything else, and if you're trying with complete acceptance of his will, you wouldn't be breaking your promise at all."

That was a surprise to her. She just thought for a minute. Then she opened her eyes. She'd been crying while we talked, and she said,

"Are you sure, Jim?"

And I said, "Yes, I'm sure."

And she said, well, if I was sure, she'd try. She started to smile, and we started to talk about something else. For years, we never mentioned it again, but I knew how she wanted her funeral.

∽

My earliest memory of prayer is the family rosary. In the living room was a picture of the Sacred Heart of Jesus. Around it were the twelve promises Jesus made to St. Margaret Mary Alocoque in the seventeenth century. One of them was that in any home where an image of his Sacred Heart was exposed and venerated, Jesus would bless those who dwell there with peace. And we were really "dwelling" on Pine Avenue! Any priest devoted to the Sacred Heart would be blessed with the power of touching even the most hardened souls. Those who would receive Holy Communion on nine successive First Fridays for the reparation of sins against Jesus in the Blessed Sacrament would have the grace of a happy death. When we said the rosary we knelt at chairs, facing the picture of the Sacred Heart, and Dad would lead. He'd name intentions that were especially impor-tant—like if Gramma was sick or somebody was out of work, or if we needed a new tenant by April 1. I didn't know what a tenant was, but I knew we needed one. Then we'd ask Mary to pray for us sinners now and at the hour of our death. Amen.

Father Heibel knew that I had said from the first grade that I wanted to be a priest. Most of the boys did then. Our understanding came from our inhaling the ways of the people who surrounded us more than from the classes, where, from first grade we memorized answers from a book called the *Baltimore Catechism #1*. Outside of class Father Heibel told me that if I ever became a priest, I should always be good to the sick and the old because that's what the parish needed most. And the people would be grateful. When I was in eighth grade, Father Danielson suggested that I go to a high school seminary in Ohio, since there was none in Erie. Dad just said no. Partly, he said, it was because I was too young to know what I wanted. But the main reason was that he couldn't think of any situation where I'd get better preparation for being a good priest than living at home.

On cold winter mornings when we came out of our bedroom, a big wood and coal fire would be going in the combination stove in the kitchen. Even on those days we'd get to school early and march over to the church for the eight o'clock Mass. Sundays, beside Mass, we'd go for Latin Vespers and Benediction. No one thought that was a lot; that was just the way we did things. I learned some of the Latin prayers of the altar boy at summer camp. Although I was soon serving on the altar, saying those same prayers, I didn't feel free there as I did in the country. At the altar I was always afraid of making mistakes.

Years later I read James Joyce's *Portrait of the Artist as a Young Man*. Many of the forms of reverence for the priests, the altar, the chalice, the Mass, and the Communion of Saints that Stephen Dedalus imbibed were part of my own experience as a boy. But Joyce lost his faith. It seemed to me that the hardness and the injustice of the Jesuits that were part of his life at school and at home just kept stretching his faith till it broke. There was simply not enough love and goodness in those who embodied the faith to protect him. The priests in our parish helped us as students, or servers, or scouts, or just friends. They were good men, so good to us. The way they lived, the way Mom and Dad and their families lived, meant that what Jesus taught wasn't just a doctrine to be transmitted. It was a way of life to be acquired by breathing.

We began to call Mom "Martha," because she was always working—for us first, but then to help Minnie, who had diabetes and eventually became blind, or her sister, Hattie, who was almost deaf, or her niece, Ora, a patient at a state mental hospital. Ora was a very beautiful girl who married happily but lost her first child in childbirth. She suffered a mental breakdown and never recovered. She was Hattie's daughter, but Hattie couldn't handle the trip and every so often Mom and Ora's sister, Ina, would make the trip together. Mom, like Martha, was busy about many things, but never out of proportion except that she was probably too hard on herself.

One of the happiest memories of my childhood was the conversation between Mom and Dad when he was trying to convince her of what a priest told him on retreat: to receive communion every time he went to Mass, unless there had been a serious sin. Confession a few times a year would be enough to keep him alert to his failures and help him to grow. Mom was amazed that Dad thought her so good because sometimes she got mad at the kids. Her conscience was very delicate. When she was convinced that something was God's will, there was no point in discussing it.

Dad expected us to do well, though he never threatened us. Often I heard him say, "You kids can do anything." Achievements came easily. For many of the wrong reasons, I always wanted to be first. One of the top honors of the eighth grade graduating class was the American Legion Medal. Before the class voted for it, another student offered to vote for me if I would vote for him. I agreed, but I really didn't think he was qualified for it. The fact is, I knew he didn't have a chance for it, and I wanted it and thought I deserved it. I didn't go to him and say the deal was off, though; I just voted for myself. That really didn't seem right even without the deal. When I got the award (by quite a majority), the whole thing seemed sour to me. So many people thought I was the All-American kid.

For part of a summer in high school, I worked on Uncle Con's farm. Another summer I had a job on the peninsula hauling wood, water, and garbage. After a long weekend, we'd attack a beach full of papers with spikes at the end of walking sticks. It was my first real job. It paid fifty cents an hour. When I got my first check it was for two weeks. We had no insurance at the time and Dad was still struggling with Mom's hospital bill. When I came home, I signed the check and gave it to Dad to help with the bill. He looked at me very directly and asked, "Are you sure you want to do this?" I said I did, and he said thanks. And I felt like a million.

☙

On December 7, 1941, the Japanese attacked Pearl Harbor, and within a week the United States was at war. Ugly headlines were a daily experience. Defenses on the continent of Europe crumbled before Hitler.

Winston Churchill emerged as a voice of hope. The evacuation at Dunkirk gave heart to everyone but without much promise. Some song writer promised that there would be blue birds over the white cliffs of Dover, but that seemed neither close nor certain.

I was a freshman at Gannon School of Arts and Sciences in Erie, living at home, paying my own way with a job calling bingo. Tuition was five dollars a credit. I was studying for the priesthood. The bishop wanted his seminarians to apply for exemption from military duty. To ensure that this exemption would hold, he sent Norb Wolf, whom I'd known since first grade, and several others with me to Baltimore to attempt to enter the major seminary at Paca Street.

2

Paca Street

LATE ONE EVENING, I LEFT ERIE ON THE PENNSYLVANIA RAILROAD. The platform was the place where soldiers said goodbye to their families to go off to unknown places to fight. I stood there in my black felt hat and black suit and tie, with a piece of luggage of my own. Mom, Dad, and Marie waited until the train pulled away. For awhile, I didn't want to talk. I wasn't sure how, but I knew that something was ending in my life and something was beginning. I just sat there and listened to the clicking of the wheels on the rails, and hurt.

The regular passenger cars must have been commandeered for use in transporting troops. There were no windows in the car I was riding in, except a circular porthole toward the middle of each side. Gradually the dust became a little grime on my skin and on anything I touched. I expected to sit up all night, but I had hopes that the number of passengers would be small enough so that I could put up my feet on the seat across from me. Sleep would then muffle the ride and comfort me.

There weren't many people, but sleep did not come. I couldn't see the small towns going past, but with each one there was a change in the sound of the rattling of the wheels on the rails. Somewhere in the night the ignorant armies were clashing. Walter Winchell's new slogan was supposed to give the clash meaning: "Work, fight, give/to make democracy live." But the world had already been made safe for democracy over twenty years before to the tune of "The Yanks are Coming." The job had to be done, they had said then. The job had been done in the war to end all wars. But now Ward was going to fight in another war, to do the job over again. I could postpone the seminary and go and fight too.

I got to Baltimore without any sleep. Paca Street ran through a run-down section of Baltimore with row-houses separated by some vacant lots filled with debris, and a red-light district. The seminary itself was a set of red brick buildings resembling nothing so much as an old factory. It was rimmed with a brick wall six or eight feet tall and about a foot thick. The top of the wall had broken bottles and pieces of glass cemented into it.

It was nearly suppertime when my arrangements were made, and I walked through the yard to make a visit to the chapel. It was dark. Over the entrance I could just make out the words, "The Lord is in His holy temple. Let all the earth keep silent before Him." I couldn't find any lights, so I felt my way by the sanctuary lamp. The whole place crackled with the many creaking sounds of an old building being exercised by the wind and then became hushed with peace such as I had never known. It was tinged with sadness, even loneliness, but I felt a presence that was way beyond me. I knew that Pine Avenue wasn't home anymore, and I regretted that this peace had to be protected by a brick wall lined with shattered glass like a local Maginot Line. I didn't know how to fit into the rest of the world. The mess was too big for me to untangle. But I knew I was not alone, and I knew I was not a stranger. I didn't know why, but I knew that I was home.

I didn't want to look for the lights. I didn't want to see the time. I was just there. I experienced a real presence, a prayer without thought, and I didn't want to disturb it. I was just there. And I was not alone.

Eventually, I heard the students get up from their chairs in prayer hall and head for the dining room. I caught up with them. About two hundred students all in cassocks went immediately to their places at table. We sat quietly through the meal as one of the students read from "My New Curate" by Canon Shehan. There were priests, some quite elderly, sitting at a raised table, being served by some of the students. As these waiters picked up the serving dishes, a couple of old sisters were hovering in the background.

Becoming part of this process was like moving back in time to another century. The old building itself was partially a memorial. It still housed the assembly hall where the early bishops of this country had gathered for the Third Baltimore Council. They were not scholars but missionaries in a pragmatic and Protestant country. In this very hall they had drawn up the famous catechism of answers about the sacraments, the Communion of Saints, and the authority of the Church that I had memorized in a simple form in first and second grade: *Baltimore Catechism Number 1.*

In one corner of the grounds was the cemetery, with the graves of the Sulpician priests who had come here from France after the French Revolution. They had come because it was so unfriendly for them in their own country, and because their services were so necessary to train priests for the new world that was emerging after the American Revolution.

My roommate was a few years older than I—I was the youngest there— and our room was in the oldest part of the building, with ceilings about fourteen feet high and long narrow rooms like bowling alleys. Between our beds, like a prop from an old Western, was a wooden washstand. On top were a large bowl for washing and shaving, a pitcher, and two soap dishes. Below was a bucket for carting water. We each had a desk and a standing closet. Because I was starting in mid-year, I didn't have the rules yet, but I knew we were supposed to be quiet, especially after supper, and completely after nine o'clock. That was when the "grand silence" began. It lasted till after Mass in the morning.

I fell asleep wondering. The silence seemed strange.

At 5:30 in the morning, I was awakened by a crack on the door. Someone was going along the corridor, hitting each door with a gavel and shouting *"Benedicamus Domino,"* to which John Murray answered, *"Deo Gratias."* I knew enough Latin to realize that when someone said, "Let us bless the Lord," I could respond, "Thanks be to God." Thirty minutes later, dressed in cassock and surplice, I was in prayer hall with two hundred other students for morning prayer.

CO

The structure of our day was strict:

> meditation
> community Mass
> part of a second Mass for Thanksgiving
> breakfast
> forty-five minute break for room cleaning and
>   preparation for class
> classes all morning
> short break for personal needs
> twenty minutes in prayer hall for reading scripture
> lunch
> break for exercise and recreation
> time for study and another class or two
> twenty-minute break for rosary
> half hour for conference or spiritual reading
> supper
> short break
> two hours for study
> lights out at ten o'clock

As the schedule came to life, so did I, in ways I couldn't have imagined.

We were supposed to "meditate" for thirty minutes each day. That was all well and good—but how exactly do you meditate? Father Dyer, affectionately called "Piggy" by the students, was my spiritual director. Having spent years in business and then in the Navy before going into the seminary, he had a matter-of-fact desire to help with the formation of matter-of-fact clergy. When I asked about meditation, he explained the difference between the Sulpician and the Ignatian method. I am not sure that he didn't confuse them. I am not sure that I could do it now without confusing them. But "methods" of meditating didn't help. What did help was St. Benedict's *Lectio Divina*—just the slow, thoughtful reading of scripture, trying to digest its richness as a cow chews its cud, without any obligation to arrive at novel insights or eloquent words.

As I began the practice of meditation, I began to feel real anxiety. I had no difficulty believing in Jesus, but I had great difficulty believing in myself. My own moral and spiritual life was complicated by my desire to please and by my fear of disappointing. My achievements seemed central to my parents' love for me and central to my relationship to God. The fear of rejection by God and by people plagued me, stirred up in me an earnestness that I had to *do more,* to achieve more—to please God, to please Mom and Dad, to please myself.

One time my worry about a situation drove me to Father Dyer, not for my weekly confession but for an additional confession that I thought I needed. He listened very patiently—not patronizingly but patiently. When I finished, he said,

"You know, what I think you need most is Navy Rule Number Six."

"What's that?"

"Don't take yourself too damned seriously."

I was stung. It wasn't simply neurotic pressure or a passing effect of having too much time for self-examination. I really felt myself disintegrating.

One evening, back at the seminary, as I continued carrying my worries with me, Father McDonald, the seminary rector, gave a quiet talk about using God's gifts: begin where you are, and use today the gifts you have at the point to which they have been developed. "Do your best; the angels can do no more." I relaxed and began to smile. I was doing as much as the angels, and I was worried about it.

∞

When I did get home on an occasional vacation, things were changing under the pressure of World War II. Ward was away at school. Marie was secretary to Archbishop Gannon. When I left, it was a further assurance that the family as we had known it was coming to an end.

The Central Depot got to be the center of a continuing drama of separations. At first, as I left, there would be only a few soldiers or sailors, their wives and families talking nervously as they waited for the train, trying to find things to chat about that weren't too serious. When the train arrived, there would be tearful hugs of people who didn't want to let go, knowing that especially in time of war any goodbye could be the last goodbye. In the years ahead, as Ward went off to duty on a destroyer in the Pacific, island-hopping back toward Japan, or when Jack was home for a furlough between trips of convoy duty on a U–Boat-infested Atlantic, the departures were heartbreaking. Bob went to the Navy next, then Tom.

Jack, especially, would be as delighted as a child to get home. Three or four days before he left, however, he would be depressed; he just couldn't shake it. Each departure brought Mom and Dad and Marie to the station. Once, when I was home and Jack was leaving, not one person talked all the way home from the station. At home, Dad tried to read. Mom got out some ironing. Marie started to ask Dad some questions to release his worry. I went out to talk to Mom. After a bit she said, "Oh, I know it, Jim. I just can't let it get me. I say to Mary, 'You know there's nothing I can do for them out there. You can. Let's make an agreement. I'll trust you to care for them when they are gone. Then I can take care of Con and the others here.'"

The first time I left home the hurt wasn't nearly as painful as the later leavings would be. Each time I just sat on the train, not wanting to talk, listening to the clicking of the wheels on the rails.

∽

When I had first arrived at Paca Street, I was planted in the certainty of the parent wisdom I had brought from my home on Pine Avenue. There praying had been the only important mental activity. Now I discovered that thinking was also an important mental activity. Before long, what I read confronted the certainty of Pine Avenue. *My* certainty.

The first mental structure to stumble was time. What could be more clear, more "certain," than time? But I was shaken by Immanuel Kant's explanation that time was only a form the mind imposed on its experience. For Kant, we know only appearances; we don't know the relationship of the appearances to reality. I managed to dismiss Kant and thereby retain my hold on certainty, but I could not dismiss St. Thomas Aquinas. He too thought time was an ideal with only a foundation in reality. This brought me face to face with my own smugness: my confidence was built on the certainty that *my* insights, *my* values were right; others were reasonable and clear only insofar as they came close to *my* common sense.

I now decided that if time were not real, I was foolish to serve it. I no longer ran up stairs to save it. Its tyranny was based on lies. The only honest thing to do was to crush its head with my heel. That was liberating.

So much for time, but when the principle of cause and effect came under assault, and with it the certainty of Aquinas's arguments for the existence of God, things were not so simply resolved. This was not a mere textbook scrimmage. For the first time in my life, my faith was shaken and I was terrified.

"Temptations against faith." Even to call what I was experiencing "temptations" was to presume that the questioner accepted God and was in touch with God; only his hold on reality was being threatened. The answer, then, was quite simple: "Hold on." But was this what I had been taught to call a "temptation," or was it an invitation to move out into fuller truth?

∞

As my hold on the foundation of what I believed slipped away, I was being drawn beyond my Pine Avenue experience of the liturgy—from the strong "Holy God We Praise Thy Name" of Christmas Mass to the mystery of Gregorian chant.

When the Sulpicians came from France to Baltimore, they brought with them the musical traditions of a Benedictine monastery planted on the River Sarthe in western France—the monastery of St. Peter of Solesmes. For a hundred years the monks there had chanted a pure form of the ancient Gregorian chant, brushed clean of the baroque additions that had cluttered it. One of the priests who came from Solesmes trained Father Eugene Walsh, who directed our choir. As I entered into the rhythm of the lives of monks in an old world and another century, I found I was able to rest from my intellectual struggles and doubts, to be bathed in the haunting power of the simple chants.

I was coming to a new love of the liturgy. The choir carried any Mass to great heights. Gradually, very gradually, I was able to find my way around the *Liber Usualis* and share in singing the *Kyrie*, the *Gloria*, the *Credo*, the *Sanctus*, and the beautiful chants of the psalms at Vespers. They were all in Latin, but by then I understood what we were singing. On a feast of Our Lady, Joe Brennan's voice just hung there in the middle of the congregation: "*Ego quasi rosa plantata super rivos aquarum fruc-tificavi.*" Joe's voice was pure Irish tenor: strong, unfaltering, honest. And he let Mary speak through it. "Like a rose planted near running water, I have brought forth fruit."

As I was drawn more and more into the liturgies of the Church year and away from the old "certain" patterns that were crumbling, I entered into a new way of measuring time. And Lent, in its starkness, came home. During Holy Week we walked to the Baltimore cathedral in cassocks and birettas. The children in the streets stared curiously, and wondered if we were coming from the "priest factory." The cathedral was cavernous, poorly lighted, and heavy in architecture. Toward the ceiling, the huge red hat of Cardinal Gibbons was suspended upside down, and well into the process of decay. But the seminary choir, and the rest of us as chorus, brought Holy Thursday, Good Friday, and Easter to a life that was real and haunting.

The Gregorian chant lamentations for the *Tenebrae* service were musically unprecedented in my experience. After each psalm or reading, another candle would be extinguished. The heaviness and darkness gradually enveloped us, but they were more than a mood. They were an honest statement of Christ's broken heart in the presence of the ruins of Jerusalem. It was Jesus, weeping over a city that refused to be gathered on the day of its visitation. It was the heart of Mary as she held the disfigured body of Jesus. At the end, we were silent with the echoes dying away in the darkened church.

∽

The summer of that year, 1943, was the last time I lived on Pine Avenue. Because I was a bit thinner than when I left, Mom would get an eggnog ready once or twice a day. The love and concern were there, but I didn't fit. I could be part of any family situation quite easily, but with visitors, after about an hour of the old conversations, I was worn out. I needed quiet. I was reading Thomas à Kempis's *Imitation of Christ,* and sometimes I'd go to the bedroom to withdraw a little from the radio or the visitors coming and going. Mom would worry that something was wrong, but I really didn't know how to share the anxieties I was dealing with. To open them to Dad or Mom or even to Marie would have been unfair. St. Alphonsus did not want seminarians to go home. "The air of home is poison," he said. I think he was speaking of the danger of falling into old behavior patterns. I knew the experience I was having was not poisonous. I knew there were not two me's, one that could be at ease in each of the worlds I lived in. Something had to bring them together.

It was easy to go to Mass each day and stay for a thanksgiving. On Sunday, I'd stay for two or three Masses. Some of the sermons left a great deal to be desired. Some of the singing was positively foolish, but I was gradually moving into a love of the Mass that was deeper than ritual splendor. I could walk to St. John's church or to the chapel at St. Mary's Home and just be with the Blessed Sacrament. If the family needed any explanation, they seemed at ease when I said I was at church, as though it was quite normal for a seminarian to be caught up in some mystery of prayer.

I was glad when September came. I was going back to men who had become friends of mine quickly, because for the first time in my life I had time for friends. In high school I had had a paper route that took me away from school right after class, so I had no time for friends. I was coming to enjoy the long recreation of an evening when we could sit around the quadrangle or walk the brick sidewalks that were sheltered by roofs from the rainy Baltimore winters.

And, for the first time, I had a private room. This one was smaller than a bowling alley, with an eight-foot window that overlooked the quadrangle and the statue of Our Lady. A desk, a crucifix, a statue of Our Lady Seat of Wisdom, a standing closet, a bed, a desk, a washstand and bowl, and it was mine. I bought a mirror for shaving and some plaid cloth for a drape.

Then I began the hardest period of my life.

I was no longer able to deal with my anxieties as passing "scruples." My struggle with faith was almost overpowering. My life seemed shallow, hypocritical. Most of what I'd called virtue was a vicious self-centeredness. Refraining from brutality, or from drunkenness or impurity—my arms-length distancing from anything that was immodest—was not a matter of loving God, or of loving anyone. It was sheer vanity. Those things were beneath me. I was too good for them. I could look back and see that my desire for the priesthood was based on that same shallowness, a desire for approval. I had tried for years to believe that my "virtue" made me acceptable to God even when I tried to hide my inner failings from myself. When I came to the seminary I had some romantic notions that it would change me and then I would change the world and we would live happily ever after. My "vocation" was built on dishonesty.

For about three months I watched myself live. There were times that I came away even from taking meals without the least recollection of what had been discussed. That three-month period was the only time in my life that I did not want to be a priest. I simply accepted the fact that I did not have the qualifications needed for the priesthood. Much more starkly, I felt that I was unable to love. It was like denying that I was real; it was certainly denying that God was real. I had to accept the awareness that five good arguments that might make the intellect comfortable by proving God's existence could accomplish no more than a ping-pong game. It was then that I realized my notion that my family accepted me because of my achievements—and so did God. In truth, I was denying their love for me—and his.

My whole world was falling apart.

And that is when the whole world changed.

I gave up the priesthood because I knew I would not be an honest priest. For years that had been my major motivation. With great pain and with much grace, and without the help of reading Saint Ignatius Loyola, I had come to a passionate indifference to the means by which I served God. Internally I gave up the priesthood and was willing to accept the tremendous disappointment this would cause my parents and friends. I made no effort to figure out what would come next. I didn't care. I made a general confession. I had gotten a copy of the newly translated Confraternity New Testament and was reading it daily. My life honestly became a kind of going into scripture with all the burdens, and coming back with all the insights. Evenings I would go out into the quadrangle under stars that were as lovely in a red-light district as anywhere. The pedestal of Our Lady's statue carried an inscription drawn from St. Bernard of Clairvaux. "God has willed to give us all things through Mary." In such an embrace my own littleness was not frightening. I did not have to prove anything.

I spent long periods of time in prayer. It wasn't discursive. It wasn't aimed at forming convictions. It was wordless. It was communion—heart to heart with Christ. I knew his love. I knew he wanted me in the seminary. I didn't know whether he wanted me to be a priest, but that didn't matter much. He was the shepherd. He knew how to manifest his will. He was also the sheep gate. Those who came through him could go in and out easily.

During those evenings when it was quiet and others were studying and I'd go alone into the quadrangle, I had the deepest sense of the love with which God loved me and almost an indifference to the future, except insofar as God would be there and his will would be accomplished and it would be beautiful. Through all the pain, what had been born were the simplest detachment and the realization that Jesus was Lord, and that in being emptied, I could receive his Spirit.

∞

One evening, I was alone in the darkness of the quadrangle. The tall trees were mainly in shadow, except as they reflected the light that was focused on the statue of Our Lady. The city noises were muffled. The other seminarians were inside, studying or asleep. I was alone, in my solitude, but I knew vividly that I was being fully embraced by God—by the Father who made me in his image and could still see that image despite the dust that had gathered, and the Son who wanted me just for himself, and then possibly for his priesthood, and the Spirit that I was just coming to know.

I am not sure how long I was held in so stupendous a peace. I knew nothing of the charismatic movement, which had not as yet touched the Catholic Church with any force. Baptism in the Spirit was not a common term theologically, but it was then that I was baptized in the Spirit. It was then that I realized that if Jesus loved me and called me, he could bring me, with all my warts, to do anything he wanted. It was no negotiation, just an awareness of being surrounded by his love and bathed in his Spirit.

The next day in prayer hall, I picked up the New Testament and began to read the fourteenth chapter of John's Gospel. I remember the thought as though it was yesterday. I wondered, "Why didn't anyone ever tell me about this before?"

I was warmly nourished as I read,

Let not your heart be troubled or be afraid. In my Father's house there are many mansions, and if I go I will prepare a place for you and I will come again and take you to myself that where I am you also may be.

My hand was trembling as the wisdom and the power of God touched me. I fell in love with John's Gospel. Chapters 14 to 17 to me opened the heart of Christ. They seemed to me to be the heart of the Bible.

I recalled later how the life of St. Augustine was changed when in response to a mysterious voice, he opened the epistles of Paul to Romans 13:

> Let us then lay aside the works of darkness and put on the armor of light; let us live honorably as in the day, not in revelling and drunkenness, not in debauchery and licentiousness, not in quarrelling and jealousy. Instead put on the Lord Jesus Christ and make no provision for the flesh, to gratify its desires.

He was able to shake off the past and move into an honest Christianity. I even wondered fancifully what a different course my life would have taken if I had been led to Paul rather than to John. But I was led to the intimacy of John. And at that time all I knew was that John was leading me to Jesus.

When Christmas came, the first I had ever spent away from Pine Avenue. It was the most splendid Christmas of my life. The Masses and the Office rejoiced because, "A child has been given to us; A Son has been born for us." For dessert we had Baked Alaska, which I had never seen before. At recreation, no one seemed homesick. When all the excitement was over, I just went to chapel to be with the Blessed Sacrament, to be grateful to God and spend time with him.

It is difficult to describe the beauty of those days. There was so much that deserved attention that I was jealous of my consciousness as it came alive. It was easy to live fully in each minute. Never had I been able to be so fully present to any event, to any person.

Now the old seminary is torn down. It was a fire hazard. Only the chapel, a historic landmark, remains. The empty niches are still there in front of the building, waiting for the perfect seminarian, who has never arrived, and Habakkuk's words still speak to all who will listen:

"The Lord is in His holy temple. Let all the earth keep silent before Him."

3

A Church with Twelve Altars

∞

AFTER I FINISHED MY PHILOSOPHY COURSE AT ST. MARY'S, Bishop Gannon transferred me to Catholic University in Washington for theology courses and for graduate English to prepare for teaching at Gannon. In June 1944, when I arrived at the university, I found a large, rolling campus with massive buildings, rimmed with religious houses of many different orders. As a child I had once visited the National Shrine of the Immaculate Conception located right there on campus. I was most impressed by the beauty and size of the crypt. Inside it was quiet, resplendent in varicolored marble from all over the world. But outside, the shrine was covered with ugly swatches of black tar paper as it waited for the money and the resolution to complete it. When I arrived in 1944 it was still the same, looking like a newly built bomb shelter.

Across from it was the Sulpician seminary—newer and brighter than Paca Street but also incomplete. Since the rooms of the seminary were full, I moved into the Casa, a small home managed by the Sulpicians. Father Carleton Sage was in charge of the house. He became my spiritual director. A convert to the Catholic Church, a professor of history, he was utterly innocent of anything scintillating, loyal to prayer, and awkward in any social situation. The university was much busier than Paca Street, with bishops coming and going. As one priest described it, "This is the only seminary in the world that is always in the process of getting back to normal." And "normal" was busy. I felt that I could have lost years of my life in that bustling atmosphere if I hadn't first had the quiet of the novitiate at Paca Street and the comfort of sitting in the small courtyard near the statue of Mary, where I'd come to Christ. Here we studied theology in a building where the chapel had twelve side altars beside the main altar. To say the daily Mass individually—a necessity, since concelebration was not in use—priests had to take turns at the side altars.

I had anticipated finding stimulating teachers in Washington, D.C. I found them in my English courses but not in theology. Our dogma teacher was still reading notes he had made years before, quoted from the long defunct *Literary Digest.* Our moral theology professor was a legalist and a casuist, utterly incapable of prudential judgment. Our scripture professor, Doctor Weisengoff, read his notes almost without comment.

Like many others at that time, Doctor Weisengoff feared being accused of "modernism." Early in the century a Sulpician father had stirred conflict in the community with his efforts to teach modern social sciences in the seminary and his belief that modern methods of scholarship should be applied to the study of scripture. It had led to a confrontation with the hierarchy and the dismissal of "modernist" priests. Dr. Weisengoff, still smarting from the memory of that episode, shielded himself from being quoted in any way that might even suggest the suppressed views. He passed out notes limited to such struggles as whether Jonah's whale was real.

The head of the department was Dr. Clifford Fenton, a huge man who came to class in cassock and always tipped his biretta when he mentioned Jesus. The editor of the *Ecclesiastic Review,* he was a friend to many bishops. With a broad New England accent, "Butch" Fenton, as he was known on campus, assumed that we would find security in his viewpoints and criticized sarcastically anyone who disagreed with him. He defended "the American Church" powerfully against a controversial book at the time, John Hugo's *Christianity in the Marketplace,* which criticized clergy more dedicated to the fringe benefits of ministry than to preaching the gospel to the poor. "You men are the cream of the Catholic youth of this country," he told us, which stirred in me concern about the Church.

At the same time, I was forming some of the strongest bondings of my life. I was getting to know and live with deacons, young men in their last year of preparation for priesthood. I watched them practicing to say Mass, heard some of their early sermons, talked with them after they came back from helping in parishes on weekends. And the experience of making real friendships, unknown before Paca Street, continued. Larry Keiffer, with a giraffe-like height and face and unpretentious common sense; Paul Berg with a powerful mind, a great deal of self-deprecation, and a faith like rock; Frank Granger, always questioning, never seeking to be center stage, completely loyal. We were young and hopeful. Our sharing was an honest joy. As we spoke about the limits of our teachers, we were able to see them as part of a church that was struggling.

In the complex intellectual climate, a part of the piety of Pine Avenue appeared in a new light. Mom would not go a day or be at ease without praying for each of us—especially for Ward, in danger in the Pacific, and Jack, in danger in the Atlantic. She asked Mary to protect them. When I began to grow intellectually, I first considered Mom and Dad's devotion to Mary a bit quaint. Gradually it came to me that the men at Catholic University who were simplest about Mary were also the ones most in love with the Blessed Sacrament, with the liturgy, with the Church. Gradually the Communion of Saints was moving out of the realm of an ideal image belonging to that earlier world. The intellectual philosophy that crippled me at Paca Street was giving way to the human response of simple people to Mary over the centuries. The "Communion of Saints" was coming to life in a real connectedness between Mom and Mary and Jack and Ward—and me.

∞

I was ripe to read the *Confessions* of Augustine. I saw myself in his struggles, but was stunned by how much *more* he saw of himself, and of Christ. When I came to this passage I was completely arrested by the voice of a man who prayed from his heart:

> Too late have I loved you, O Beauty so ancient and so new, too late have I loved you! Behold, you were within me, while I was outside: it was there that I sought you, and, a deformed creature, rushed headlong upon these things of beauty which you have made. You were with me, but I was not with you. They kept me far from you, those fair things which, if they were not in you, would not exist at all. You have called to me, and have cried

out, and have shattered my deafness. You have blazed forth with light, and
have shone upon me, and you have put my blindness to flight! You have
sent forth fragrance, and I have drawn in my breath, and I pant after you.
I have tasted you, and I hunger and thirst after you. You have touched me,
and I have burned for your peace. (book 10, chap. 27; Image ed., 1960)

I began to realize that because Augustine could *see* more than I, he could
respond more to Christ.

When Dr. Lilly, the translator of the Acts of the Apostles for the Confraternity edition of the New Testament, arrived at Catholic University, he
breathed fresh air into theology. He had us read Joseph Hoisner's *Paul
of Tarsus* and Ferdinand Prat's *The Epistles of Paul,* which prepared me
for another important step: reading the epistles not merely to understand
Paul's theology intellectually but to enter into and begin to grasp his *consciousness,* and in doing so, to become more aware of the mental outlook
that shaped me. All the bits of parent wisdom that had once given him
religious security—that he was a Jew of the tribe of Benjamin and a strict
keeper of the Law—now fell before his response to Christ, who died the
most shameful death for a Jew: on a stake, outside the gates of the holy
city Jerusalem. When Paul said "Life means Christ" he was describing not
an argument or a new perspective on his old ways, but what held his own
experience together. In Paul, I recognized with surprise an ancient frame-
work of my own disintegration and coming to new life.

Now I was awakened to the excitement of the epistles themselves. It
was powerful for me to grasp that behind the Epistle I could realize the
presence of God, and the real amazement of Paul, who was writing not
simply of what God does, but of what Christ was doing in him. Paul had
to be a richly alive human being in order to write:

This, then, is what I pray, kneeling before the Father, from whom every
fatherhood in heaven or on earth, takes its name. In the abundance of his
glory may he, through his Spirit, enable you to grow firm in power with
regard to your inner self, so that Christ may live in your hearts through
faith, and then planted in love and built on love, with all God's holy people you will have the strength to grasp the breadth and the length, the
height and the depth; so that, knowing the love of Christ, which is beyond

knowledge, you may be filled with the utter fullness of God. (Eph. 3:14–19
[*New Jerusalem Bible*])

Through Paul I grasped clearly that the struggles that accompanied
my stepping beyond the mental patterns of the parent wisdom could not
be resolved in newer, more sophisticated intellectual positions. I had to
enter, like Paul, into a realization that the Word dwelled among us. It did
not just instruct us. This Word *dwelled* among us.

∽

The National Shrine became an increasingly important part of my life.
There we had our Sunday liturgies; there we joined many others from
other religious orders, becoming a worshiping community—and that was
when we were most fully ourselves. There, at the time of the designation
of St. Anthony as a Doctor of the Church, Cardinal Cushing asked us for
the faith and trust that would make it possible for us to preach to the
birds. There I received tonsure from an old bishop who cut off a few
strands of my hair and made me a cleric, asking me to realize that the
Lord himself was my inheritance. There I spent time in quiet prayer, and
there, as I looked around at the altars in the many chapels built with
different-colored stone from all over the world, I felt a part of the shared
belief of the people who had knelt before altars for centuries, and I knew
that the whole thing was too beautiful not to finish.

It was at the shrine also that I received the minor orders of lector,
porter, acolyte, and exorcist. Each time we prepared for any order, we
were questioned about our faith and our intentions. The orders could be
requested only by someone who had the priesthood in view. Almost every
time I was at home, Mom would ask me if I was sure. Always I would tell
her that I wasn't sure I'd be a priest, but I was sure God wanted me in the
seminary and I wanted to be there. That always worried her. It was no
worry for me. The old sense of striving to be complete in a preconceived
image—even that of "priest"—had given way to the clear and simple sense
that the Lord was leading me where I was, at that moment. I knew if he
wanted my priesthood I would arrive there, not by a tremendous act of
determined willpower but by following a step at a time.

On May 9, 1945, we greeted the news that the war was over in Europe by a large gathering of priests, brothers, sisters, and seminarians at the shrine singing the magnificent "Te Deum." Three months later, on August 15, the Feast of the Assumption, we gathered again. The fighting was now over in the Pacific too. The war was over.

One free day a few of us took the train down to Harper's Ferry. I can still remember climbing up a small mountain, finding a patch of ripe blueberries, and sitting in the middle of them. A hawk below me was soaring over the old railroad station and the old farms. Morning's minion; kingdom of daylight's dolphin. The sky was a perfect blue. The war was over. My chief responsibility for the moment was to breathe. I didn't realize until then how much the war had been part of my life and mood for four years. But the war was over now, and Jack and Ward and Bob and Tom were all safe. Something in that spoke about Mary. At least it did to Mom and Dad.

∞

In the spring of 1946 I was scheduled to receive the subdeaconate, the step toward priesthood in which one takes a vow of reciting the Divine Office daily for life, and a vow of celibacy. I was twenty-two years old. I didn't think of a vow as provisional or reversible. Nor did I feel any special obligation to agonize over the life-timeness of it. I wouldn't dignify a long time into being the real enemy when I knew that time was not real. I had no fear that it would open to a loveless life. I believed Paul when he said that a person who forgoes marriage for the gospel has the highest life possible for a Christian. Jesus made love the heart of all ministry. I viewed celibacy, therefore, as the life of the greatest love possible for a Christian—if Christ called a person to it.

But I would also be cutting the long, thin thread of life that had come down to me through the centuries and wouldn't be passed on. I was convinced that I didn't have to beget children in order to love. In the tuberculosis sanitarium I was visiting regularly there were many people who believed that no one would treat them with an honest love.

What I thought of most, I suppose, was never having any human being I could regard as "my own." It would be un-Christian to build up an artificial family. "These are mine." "She is mine." "Hands off!" They would eventually go away to where their lives were properly centered, and humanly, I would be alone. If Christ accepted my vow of celibacy, filling in that void would be his responsibility. Yet I knew many people in vows who didn't seem joyful. I went through a mental review of the pastors I had known in Erie. I had often thought, "I hope I don't wind up like that. I hope that doesn't happen to me." I decided it was simply a matter of how much I could trust Christ.

Dad and Mom drove down for the ceremony of my becoming a sub-deacon. Mom wasn't a traveler, but this was important. The crypt of the shrine was splendid. The liturgy was splendid. But even without the splendor, whatever good happened to any of us made them joyful. They had never seen Washington, so that afternoon we went sightseeing. Dad was driving and Mom was sitting next to him in the front seat. That was always her place. She never learned to drive. With each new car she learned where the emergency brake was and how to pull it if anything happened to Dad when he was driving. In fact, the emergency brake was one of the few things that came between them.

After the Capitol, the Supreme Court, the Washington Monument, the Lincoln Shrine, and a bit of the Smithsonian, we just went riding to look at the buildings and the parks. In the back seat, I fell asleep. When I awakened they were talking and didn't realize that I was no longer asleep. They weren't discussing anything very important, but it belonged entirely to the two of them. They shared so gently and had so much in communion. I felt a terrible pang of loneliness. That was what I had vowed to give up.

But then, this was what Christ had promised to fill up.

∞

The Divine Office I had vowed to recite daily was a joy. It was still in Latin. I used the diocesan priest's breviary, which pulled together parts of huge volumes that were used by monks as they gathered publicly to pray and to chant the psalms—morning, noon, late afternoon, and evening as they had for hundreds of years. The lengthy excerpts from the scriptures arranged in a psalter for chanting allowed me each day to enter this extended community of prayer—to connect with other communities around the world who were praying the same prayer at the same time of day.

I felt such a strong attraction to monastic life, in fact, that I spent some time at the Trappist monastery in Gethsemani, Kentucky. I loved the quiet, the peace, and the shared liturgy, and I began reading the history of monasticism. As the words of the song suggested, holiness seemed to be there, "in a monastery garden." In an unusual permission, Father MacDonald said I might get up an hour early every day to be in chapel.

This was the path that led out of the inner turmoil caused by the collapse of my mental certainty. As I followed it, I found the writers who could help me formulate some new mental patterns. The philosopher Jacques Maritain was a great help to me. What impressed me was his view that the master goes to the *simple roots* of knowledge. The lesser thinker adds more and more knowledge, which leads to multiplicity without awareness of the simple, unified source.

In learning to pray, I had found that methods of meditation, too, could generate multiplicity. I had gotten hold of new translations by Allison Piers of Teresa of Avila and *The Complete Works of John of the Cross*. I read about the contemplative experience and wondered. As I was drawn more and more to the simple—in daily life, in reading, in people—I stumbled on Thérèse of Lisieux's *Story of a Soul*. She was only twenty-four when she died, and was "too little" to follow the path of great mortifications—the path of the great Carmelite founders. In a clear trusting voice Thérèse spoke of the everyday providence of God. When she prayed, she spoke as simply to Jesus as if he were right there with her. "O Jesus! . . . I feel that if You found a soul weaker and littler than mine. . . . You would be pleased to grant it still greater favors, provided it abandoned itself with total confidence in Your Infinite Mercy."

In the fall of 1946 I became a deacon and knew the excitement of my first distribution of Holy Communion, and the excitement of rehearsing the rubrics of the Mass. But with it came a growing dread of the active ministry. As a deacon, I had taken the final step before the priesthood, and it seemed that giving up my quiet and simple time for prayer and study would be too great a loss to face.

I had come to a deep sense of the holy in prayer—a kind of fulfillment of the promise I'd experienced that first night in the chapel at Paca Street when I was alone with the Blessed Sacrament. I knew that as a priest I would do my duty, but I was afraid that I would resent people for interfering with my interior life. To hold onto that interior quiet I wanted another year before ordination. Since I was only twenty-three, I had to be given a dispensation to be ordained—canonically I should be at least twenty-four. I didn't want a dispensation. I wanted to wait, but my friends would have none of it. Neither would Father Sage. So it didn't happen.

At the seminary, whenever one of the deacons left for ordination, the whole community would gather at the door and sing. "Ecce quam bonum"—"Behold how good it is for brethren to dwell together in one." I had shared that often as one who sang. Then in May, two days before ordination, it was over. Norb Wolf and I were at the door with our bags packed, and the song rose around us. How good it is.

4

*Huge Bodies
and a Little Book*

ORDINATION WAS PLANNED FOR ST. PETER'S CATHEDRAL IN MY
hometown of Erie. I arrived a day early with the eleven others to be
ordained and we went to St. Mark's seminary. We were not to go to our
homes. St. Mark's was housed in an old factorylike building on East Third
Street, where it had once done years of service as an orphanage. To the
seminarians who lived there, we were celebrities. In the afternoon I
walked out to the Villa Motherhouse to see Marie. She was now Sister
Gertrude Marie, a Sister of St. Joseph entrenched in a stern, floor-length
black-and-white habit; much of her head was covered. But, as always, her
eyes gave permission to be. When I walked back to the seminary I headed
to chapel, just to be there for awhile. I was saying yes to God, but I was
crying at the price of it.

The next morning, the cathedral was ablaze in splendor. There was a
huge procession of boy scouts, altar boys, and I guess a marching band or
two—all the things that Mom didn't want at her funeral. The congregation
was asked to come forward if they had any objection to the ordination of
any one of us. The seminary rector said that as far as was humanly possible to ascertain, we were ready. Then each of us was called by name. No
speech. Just one step forward and the word, *"Adsum."* Here I am.

It goes all the way back to Samuel, who, when he heard a voice calling
his name answered, "Here I am" (1 Sam. 3:4). But Samuel, lying in the
sanctuary near the ark, didn't know it was the voice of the Lord; he didn't

know how to respond and ran to old Eli "whose eyes were beginning to grow dim." Eli "understood that God was calling the child." He told Samuel, if he heard the voice again, he should say, "Speak, Lord, for your servant is listening." I wondered why God wanted to involve people, who mixed things up, in helping others to respond to him. Only now I was closer to Jesus. "Here I am, Lord. I come to do your will. You were not pleased by holocausts or sin offerings; a body you have fitted to me." I come.

Then we were prostrate on the floor. The choir and the congregation called on all the saints to intercede for us. Peter, Andrew, James, John, Paul, Augustine, Francis, Dominic. All the martyrs and confessors, the holy men and women of the past. The bishop laid hands on me, and all the priests there imposed hands in testimony. I promised obedience and stood with the bishop and the priests and the other eleven newly ordained, and concelebrated Mass.

For days I blessed everyone and everything, but mainly God. I was embarrassed by the many people who were aware of me and gracious to me. Such reverence for priesthood; there must have been many great men in the past, I thought, who lived the priesthood reverently, in a way that consoled them.

∽

I was assigned to assist Father Raymond Geiger at Blessed Sacrament parish at the edge of town. It had no church yet. The school had been built first with a gym that would serve as a church for a few years. And Sister Gertrude Marie was its principal. The weekend after I arrived, Father Geiger left for a ten-day vacation. When I asked about my duties, he said I wouldn't need to preach—as though that would be a relief for me when I had spent years getting ready to do it. But he said it was their custom to have no sermons from May till October. I could go to the school, but I shouldn't get in the teachers' way. It was a young parish, so there weren't many sick people, but if there were any people in the hospital, I should go. I wouldn't have to count the collection or do any banking—that was all worked out. A few days a week we had no meals there, but I could get my own. There was a meeting of the women of the parish coming up the following Wednesday, and I should go to that and say something nice.

I had no idea how to handle myself at a meeting of a hundred women, but I was young and people still thought I was cute. I was timid, but I figured they would handle things for me.

There were just a few more weeks of class at the grade school. Marie assured me that I was not in the way. The children rarely had a priest in the classroom. I enjoyed every minute with them. In the first grade, I asked, "Does God have any legs?" One of the boys waved his hand furiously for attention. When I called on him, he said, "No." I asked, "How do you know?" He paused just a second and said, "What would he do with them? He's everyplace anyhow." So I knew I was not just there to give.

The Ladies' Guild meeting went easily. They were very motherly. I helped get a football team together for the grade school. They called me "coach," but were disappointed when I didn't get angry at the other teams who were allegedly using "ringers" when we ourselves were pure of heart and hands. I instructed a few couples before marriage, celebrated Mass at their weddings, and developed friendships.

∞

At 5:30 one morning I was awakened by a phone call. The woman who called asked me to come at once. Her mother was unconscious, and the doctor had told the family she was not likely to live through the day. The daughter who was calling me was an adult convert to the Church. She knew that her mother, who had been away from the Church for forty years, was really bothered by it and wanted to make peace with God. Even though I knew she was unconscious, I stopped at church and picked up the Blessed Sacrament as well as the oils. As soon as I came into the house, the daughter told me her mother had just regained consciousness. Her father, who had a very full mustache when mustaches were not common, eyed me with suspicion. Then he blurted out,

"You better tell her you're a doctor so she won't be frightened."

Without any hesitation I told him, "If you understood what Catholics believe, you'd realize she wouldn't be frightened to have a priest. She'd be glad."

When he saw I was willing to take over, he let me.

The three of us went into the bedroom. I told her I was a priest and asked her if she'd like to receive communion. She said she would but should go to confession first. The others left during the confession. Then I called them back to be present for the anointing and communion. The sick woman was radiant and proceeded to recover.

I stopped with communion several times. She told me she had been so lonesome for communion. Now she never wanted to give it up. She wanted to know whether anything could be done about her marriage. Her husband was a Lutheran; neither had ever been married before, but when they were young they decided that to avoid hassles they'd be married by a justice of the peace. She hadn't realized at the time how much the sacraments meant to her. I said that if her husband were agreeable, we could bless the marriage.

She asked, "What does that mean?"

"We'll have the marriage ceremony again, but this time with a priest and two witnesses. Do you think your husband would agree?"

She paused a minute and said, "I don't know. Will you ask him?"

I agreed and went very simply to ask him to marry his wife. I was twenty-three. He was about sixty-five. He turned red and huffed and puffed,

"Why, you're telling me all my kids are bastards."

That was the beginning. He went on from there. I didn't argue. I just sat there quietly. At last he subsided and said,

"Well, will it help my wife?"

I assured him it would.

"Well, then I'll do it for her."

I checked on procedure and arrived with some forms, one of which included his promise that future children would be baptized and raised as Catholics. His outrage started to take over again. Loudly he said,

"This is dumb."

Quietly I said, "Yes, this is dumb."

Our eyes met and he began to smile. That day we renewed their marriage promises with some artificial roses for a bouquet, a son and a daughter for witnesses—and not the least bit of tension.

She recovered. When I'd stop in, the two of them would light up as for the return of a son. Once he said to me, "I know you don't agree with the way we got married, but that way there was no quarreling or hurt feelings. In all the years, we never had one argument in our home about religion." By then I didn't have to hold back. "How many of your children go to church?" I knew the answer. Only the one daughter who had married a Catholic and had come into the church. He admitted that a bit reluctantly. While I had him on the run, I said, "You probably never had any fights in your home about jet planes either. If you don't talk about a thing, you don't quarrel about it."

We started to talk about his own soul and the need for prayer. He was gentle as a child. We became good friends. They are both dead now. I have no worry about their souls.

In those first few days when Father Geiger was away, several people stopped for baptismal certificates. I was completely humbled when, after keeping them for over an hour, I couldn't find the forms to make them out. I took their addresses and promised to send them. I had a glimpse of my future administrative genius when, after almost two full days of looking everywhere I could imagine, I couldn't find any forms at all, except applications for admittance to Saint Mary's Home for the Aged. I sat at the door and waited, but nobody came who wanted to go to St. Mary's.

A few days after Father Geiger came back from his vacation he told me that he did not want me to use his confessional in the future. I had been using it while he was away, but he told me always to use one that was for visiting priests. He gave me no explanation, but he was most emphatic. I knew the reason. Father Geiger was permissive about birth control; I was not. By degrees, it dawned on me that other priests were not preaching about it. I began to realize that though it was the "official doctrine" of the Church, the Church was not teaching it. It was not a matter of faith. With the tremendous sacrifices it could entail, I was not at all convinced that I could insist on it if it were not known to us by faith.

Father Geiger was always courteous to me, but several times I got notes from him—"Mass to be over in twenty-three minutes." That meant Sunday Mass. There were no sermons, but there was no way I could cut down to that time limit. Nor did we ever discuss it. I'd get the notes, and he must have figured that I ignored them. He told an older priest who was a friend of mine that I was too intense and probably would not last in the priesthood for more than six months before I'd have a breakdown or give the whole thing up.

At the parish the days got busier, but mornings were serene. I'd go over to church for an hour's prayer before Mass. Usually the only other person there was Anna Pulaski, who lived in a little saltbox cabin across from the temporary church.

In August I had word that I was to leave the parish and return to Catholic University to start a master's degree in English. I was to teach. I was stunned. In just a few months, I was part of the lives and families of so many people. Years before, I had made up my mind that I would not lose my heart to any assignment—not that I wouldn't love people or give everything, but I could never let my spiritual stability rest in a given situation. I had a deep admiration for John the Baptist, whom I admired as a fully dedicated man without a bit of fat on his body or in his speech. When he knew it was time to turn his disciples over to Jesus and the people thought he would be torn by a sense of competition, he said, "A man has what is allotted to him from heaven; he [Jesus] must grow more and more. I must grow less and less." But it was still hard.

In September, I went back to Catholic University. I moved into Caldwell Hall as sacristan/coordinator of the chapel. Each morning the twelve altars would be used several times by student priests. The busyness accented my desire to come back to the parish at Christmas and help out, but Father Geiger wrote that I wasn't needed.

At Christmas I stopped to visit Anna Pulaski. She was as gracious as could be; her smile lighted up the cottage where she lived. Very seriously she said,

"There's something I want to tell you, Fadder."

"What is it, Anna?"

"Last year when I saw the pictures in the paper before ordination, I looked them over and I liked yours especially. So I asked Jesus to send you here and he did. Then I thought later, it's not right to have him out here in this country parish, he should be someplace bigger. So I prayed that you'd go to a place where there would be twelve altars and twelve priests.

Only I prayed you'd come back sometimes so I could see you. And then in November the furnace broke down, and I thought 'That young priest will be over here praying early in the morning and he'll be cold, maybe even catch cold on account of me.' So I prayed you wouldn't be back . . ."

"Wait a minute, Anna," I said, and told her she was not to pray for anything else for me without my permission!

One afternoon, I drove down to North Warren to the State Hospital where my cousin Ora was a patient. She was very passive and not easily roused to conversation. I hadn't seen her for years. My memory of her was as a young and laughing bride. Now she was older, heavier, subdued, asking for directions, "Should I go now? Is this where I should sit?" Her hearing was poor, and I wasn't sure that she could place me. Before I left, she asked me to write my name and address, and I suspected she just wanted to try to figure out who I was.

A few days later I had a post card from her. She called me "Father Jim" and thanked me for coming to her. She said she was so glad the two of us could go to chapel together, and then wrote an indelible line, "While we sat there, I had a little Benediction in my heart." I left thinking her aging and unkempt, and I never guessed the beauty of her heart. "All the beauty of the king's daughter is within."

∽

The old fears of the demands of people draining my inner life were giving way little by little in simple relating to people, one at a time. People like Anna. And cousin Ora. No effort at discussion. I was learning to relate person to person—in a simpler, more direct, less tiring way. Still, the more I had of quiet and prayer, the more I craved it. My experience of the holy was most powerful in the silence of the monastery.

I made arrangements to spend a week at the Trappist abbey at Conyers, Georgia, Our Lady of the Holy Spirit. I was seriously thinking of a Trappist life. Father James Fox was abbot at the time, and he very graciously gave me permission to live with the community. He loaned me the clothes of a choir monk, gave me a bunk in the community dormitory, a stall in choir, an altar for my private Mass daily, and a place at table. It seemed like the middle of the night when we rose. We used huge books on stands for the psalter. There was no talking, but one or another of the monks would help me out of any bewilderment that registered on my face. At the end of compline, the chapel would be dark except for a ring of lights around the statue of the Blessed Virgin. In one voice out of the quiet darkness, we would sing, "Salve Regina, Mater Misericordiae." Mother of Mercy, our life, our sweetness, and our hope. Then the abbot would bless each of us with holy water as we passed his stand on the way to the dormitory, and sleep would come too fast for me to collect my thoughts. Each new morning had the same thrill of being lost in the liturgy.

Father James had his degree in business from Yale, but he was a very simple man, a very devout man. He had been novice master at Gethsemani. Eventually he returned there as abbot. When he was made novice master, he resigned in favor of St. Thérèse of Lisieux, the Little Flower, and he just helped her. At Conyers, in the novitiate library, the sections were headed Scripture, Theology, Church History, Liturgy, Canon Law, the Little Flower. During the week there I made up my mind to ask Bishop Gannon to release me from the Erie diocese so that I could enter the Trappists. The brother who drove me to the station was probably in his late forties. He had an interior quiet. He was watching me very thoughtfully, waiting for me to speak. Feeling Trappist, I said nothing. So he asked,

"What's the matter, was it more difficult than you expected?"

"No, it wasn't difficult at all. I loved it."

"Then why are you leaving?"

Only then did I realize that the abbot had made a major exception in letting me come into the community to spend these days. The others thought I had entered permanently. They had accepted me as a brother. When I explained he said, thoughtfully, "If you come back, you'll be an abbot in less than ten years." We were quiet the rest of the way.

At Easter I asked the archbishop to release me for the Trappists. He said he didn't see how anyone who knew the needs of the Erie diocese could ask to be released for somewhere else. He stood up and said, "No. I am not going to permit you to go, at least not now. And I am not going to send you back to the University. You'll come back and start teaching at Gannon. And you will also preach to the sisters. You let the superiors know you are available and make arrangements with them. When you preach, I don't want just random ideas. Your talks should be about half an hour long and *I want them written out.* We may discuss this other matter sometime, but there is no point in discussing it further now." I asked for his blessing and left.

∞

I moved into Gannon College—an all-male school—to live with students coming on newly developed football scholarships. Since we had no dormitory yet to house them, they were to live in the old gym at St. Mark's— a surplus army building close to collapse. The students would be living on the stage. I was supposed to supervise them until Gannon could acquire a "suitable facility." But I would have privacy. I could live in the ticket booth.

The students for the most part came from very poor families. Our common problems brought us together in dealings that led to lifetime friendships. I was earnest with them in regard to the need for study, but when they came home brutalized by hours of practice, they were too tired to do anything. Often their hearts were not in study, and my heart was not in pushing them. I was supervisor, uncle, and friend, though a few of them were my own age. I was twenty-four.

Sooner or later, almost all of them came to me for confession, usually a general confession. I remember one especially. I had him in class, where we were discussing Christ's doctrine of loyalty to the truth. Late one evening he came to see me to talk about his own life and asked me to explain what was meant by a general confession. I explained that "to confess" means to praise, that confession is not simply a listing of embarrassing moments but a statement of one's failures with an act of praise to Christ, that although I have done these ugly things and have these tendencies that could render me monstrous, I expect through the grace of Christ to live as a child of God. The future is more important than the past. A confession is general when instead of covering only the period of life since one's last confession, it goes over a much longer period, even one's whole lifetime.

He listened most attentively, then asked when a general confession was necessary. I told him the only time it was necessary was when one had consciously been making bad confessions by omitting things that were too difficult to say or by saying things without any sincere intention of using God's grace to change.

Quickly, he responded, "That's what I want to do."

I asked, "Do you think it's necessary?"

"Not really necessary. But in high school I used to horse around a lot, and I'd go to confession when Mom said it was time, but I'm not sure that I thought about it enough or that I tried to plan for the future."

I saw that he was not scrupulous, just beautifully honest. So I said, "If that's how you feel about it, it might be a good idea."

"How do I go about it?"

"Just think about it awhile, and then if you want, I could ask one of the other priests to go to a confessional at a particular time, if you thought confessing to a stranger would be easier."

He stammered, "Well, I kind of thought about asking you, Father, only I was afraid that after I finished, you wouldn't think very much of me."

"I certainly wouldn't want you to come to me if our friendship would make it more difficult for you. But as far as what I would think, all I can think when anything turns up in confession is how good God is, and with what marvelous humility he has blessed this person!"

I didn't tell him, but as a seminarian, I used to worry about how I would handle the seal of confession. I knew that whatever I heard was bound to stop there, and I had no fear of gossiping about it. But I knew also that I could never even use it in dealing with the penitent, never even discuss it with him unless he brought it up himself. I could never even change my attitude toward him or her. I thought that would require heroic self-control. It didn't. In hearing confessions, I found that it never even entered my mind that "you are the one who stole," or "you are the one who committed adultery." Somehow the grace of God makes it easy. "You are God's child, and you are dear to me."

When I finished describing a general confession for him, he said,

"Well, that's what I want to do. Now I'm going to take three days to get ready."

"You don't need three days. You don't have to torture yourself to save your soul. You think about it this afternoon, and I'll be here this evening. Come in sometime after nine, and we'll take care of it."

He agreed and left. That evening he came in quite nervous. "You don't know what you're getting into, Father."

"I'm not worried. Do you want me to ask questions? Or do you want to do it on your own?"

"Would you ask questions?"

I would. He opened his past with the simplicity of a child. And he opened his future. I was humbled by his innocence and by the great love of Christ. In Latin, which we were still using, I said, "I absolve you from your sins, in the name of the Father and of the Son and of the Holy Spirit." And I hugged him. The embrace of reconciliation, the bond of brothers and sisters. There is joy in heaven. There is joy on earth also.

One day I got a phone call that was different from the others. It was a man I didn't know. Without any explanation, he courteously asked for an appointment. He sounded serious and sincere; I gave him a time for meeting at my office. He arrived carrying a case full of insurance plans, which he proceeded to unfold and explain. Nothing would happen to me that wouldn't leave me better off. If I lost a hand, I'd have so much money a month for the rest of my life that I wouldn't need a hand. I was too shy to interrupt him. When he finished I said his presentation was impressive, but I wasn't interested in getting any insurance. I had a one-thousand-dollar burial policy and that was all I wanted.

Somewhat indignantly, he began to collect his materials. Then he said, "I don't want to seem insolent, but can you tell me where you could get a policy that would match this?" I said I didn't know much about insurance policies, but Jesus had said that we should take care of the poor, and promised that he would take care of us. He pulled himself up to his full height and said, "Now wait a minute. If you're talking about poverty, that's all right if you go into a religious order and take vows. Because there if anything happens to you, the order will take care of you."

I said, "Oh, is that how it works?" Then I assured him that Christ's promise was all I needed. He told me, kindly, that I was young and would learn that I had to be more practical. If I ever reconsidered and wanted his services, he'd be ready to help me. So I asked him to pray for me, and he said he would. After that I always recognized the voice and stance of an insurance man when one called. That saved me time.

By semester break, Gannon had inherited a house at 18th near Peach Street. The Nickel Plate Railroad tracks went right through the living room, or at least seemed to. As a group, we moved from the old gym to the old home. In one large bedroom we had three double bunks, but we added two toilets and showers, and adequate heat. The suitable facility had arrived for our family—all fourteen of us.

Two of the football players, Bill Gilchrist and Bob Stevenson, wanted to take instructions in order to be baptized, and I began a practice that was to go on for my whole life. I learned fairly quickly not to be intimidated by the age of any person, or the size, or the beauty or physique, or the wealth, or the smell. A few times, when we found ourselves talking about the weather or the team, I became aware that there were more important things they wanted to discuss and were fearful or shy about approaching. Once or twice I let them leave after having wasted their time and effort. Eventually, one by one, they began to open their stories to me. As they did, I paid less attention to the superficial differences; I was learning to listen and allow each one's distinct experience of life to become visible to me.

One evening I heard the chapel door close loudly and saw a young man come out and go to sit on the ledge that used to hold one of the two great lions that defended the entrance to the college. Something was raging inside of him, but I knew the situation was too intense to ask any questions, so I just wished him good evening and was there. When he wanted to talk, it became clear. In his neighborhood, there was a kindly old man whose wife had died, who had become a kind of grandfather to all the children of the area. For two days, they had not seen him. Then someone called the police, who broke in and found that he had died, seated on the commode. It bothered him that such a good man should die alone. It upset him completely that he should die in so undignified a position. Human life, in its passage, should be treated with more dignity. I had to approach gently. I asked whether he knew him well. Whether the man had any faith. Whether he believed in life after death. Each yes helped to build to that fundamental yes we need to enter into the mind of God.

And I remember well a young intern from one of the local hospitals. He was Egyptian, a Muslim, and he was most serious. Within three paragraphs of our first conversation, he said that he had heard from friends that I gave instructions and that he wanted to become a Catholic. I asked him why. He explained that, when he was a child, his family had been well-to-do. They were all Muslims, but they had a maid who was a Christian. One day she found him in an upper room in their house aiming a BB gun into an upper room of the house across the way. She grabbed the gun and asked "What are you doing?" He told her that he was going to kill a bird that belonged to the boy that lived there, because the boy had killed his cat. Muhammad said, "An eye for an eye; a tooth for a tooth." She said, "Well, if you kill his bird, he'll have to do something else to you. Anyhow he didn't kill your cat deliberately. It was an accident. Besides that, if you go on feuding, you won't have anyone to play with. If you forgive him, it will all be over in a short time. You two will be friends again."

She kept the gun. He grumbled and left, but then he went for a walk and did a great deal of thinking. When the family was at supper, he said, "I think our maid is wiser than Muhammad, because he says 'an eye for an eye' and she says we should forgive our enemies." His father made a fist and punched him so hard that he fell out of his chair. The father told him he never wanted to hear that kind of talk again. So he didn't say any more, but he thought about it and waited.

In all the pressures of family feuds and conflicts among the Arabs and the Israelis, he thought that forgiveness was the only way to peace. He knew forgiveness was not weakness. He knew the forgiveness of Jesus on the cross was a strength he wanted to approach. So much of his journey had already been made. I felt privileged to share the further journey. His baptism was a moment of great faith and deep joy. I knew his openness to God and God's love for him. I didn't know his future, but I knew it was in God's care.

∽

In those early days of my priesthood, young and not far myself from the classroom, as I began to enter into the journeys of those who came to me, I found myself developing a deepening reverence for people. There was a freshness and a splendor to everyone who came, not just the first time, but each time we were together. He or she had changed, and I had changed. I knew with those who wanted to become Catholics that I had to enter into the world they had lived in, to grasp what they were wrestling with, what they could see, and what they hoped for. Only after I knew we were sharing a good deal would I suggest any reading.

Almost always, we'd begin with scripture—never simply an instruction to read the Bible, but a cautious judgment about where this person, in his or her particular life, could enter scripture. What words would speak to them—not regurgitated but as the voice of a loving father whose word could go deep into any heart that was open. Often that meant the Acts of the Apostles and the Gospel of John. The sermons in Acts spoke so bluntly and simply that they swept away a great deal of debris that had been substituted for Christianity. I found that the conversion of Paul often led a man or woman to realize what Christ was asking:

> ... I saw a light from heaven shining more brilliantly than the sun round me and my fellow-travellers. We all fell to the ground, and I heard a voice saying to me in Hebrew, "Saul, Saul, why are you persecuting me? It is hard for you, kicking against the goad." Then I said, "Who are you, Lord?" And the Lord answered, "I am Jesus, whom you are persecuting. But get up and stand on your feet, for I have appeared to you for this reason: to appoint you as my servant and as witness of this vision in which you have seen me, and of others in which I shall appear to you. I shall rescue you from the people and from the nations to whom I send you to open their eyes, so that they may turn from darkness to light, from the dominion of Satan to God, and receive, through faith in me, forgiveness of their sins and a share in the inheritance of the sanctified. (Acts 26:13–18 [*New Jerusalem Bible*])

I had grown up believing in "the sacraments," but in these encounters with people reaching out to God from the context of their own lives, I was coming to a deeper sense of the sacramental: grace coming through everyday things and events. The Gospel of John brought home the meaning of Baptism, the Eucharist, Reconciliation, not as late-medieval traditions and not as part of a plan of God that was too broad ever to descend from the global, but something simple, personal, individual, and living:

> If you make my word your home
> you will indeed be my disciples;
> you will come to know the truth,
> and the truth will set you free.

They answered, "We are descended from Abraham and we have never been the slaves of anyone; what do you mean, 'You will be set free?'" Jesus replied:

> In all truth I tell you,
> everyone who commits sin is a slave,
> Now a slave has no permanent standing in the household,
> but a son belongs to it for ever.
> So if the Son sets you free,
> you will be indeed be free.
>
> (John 8:31–36 [*New Jerusalem Bible*])

Freedom is not just for a woman taken in adultery and in danger of stoning; freedom is an escape from lies. And, as different lies hold different people bound, each escape is different. But each new freedom is a gift from Jesus—gentle, powerful, and most individual.

Sometimes as I was stretched to respond to experiences beyond my own, and together we entered scripture, the instructions would go on for months. I never found myself being a tape recorder, or a fountainhead, or a distant oracle; rather, I was a friend and companion for the journey, waiting for God to act, knowing we were pilgrims together.

∽

Late one night a young man came to my office restless, questioning. He wanted to go for a walk, so we did. For some hours he talked to me and the night. He had a very difficult alcoholic problem and little faith with which to handle it. He had been dating a Catholic girl who was the best thing that had ever happened to him. She had told him that she knew she loved him, but she could never think of raising children with an alcoholic father. He told her he would give up drinking completely, and for a few months he did. Then he started to drink again. One evening when they were out on a date she told him it was no good to pretend, that it was over and they should say goodbye. He protested. She got out of the car.

In anger he started the car and drove off furiously. What he didn't realize was that her foot was caught in the door. He dragged her body for almost a block before he realized it. Then he rushed her to the emergency room at a Catholic hospital.

The attendants were too busy with her to pay attention to him. He was half in shock. He didn't know whether she would live or die. He wandered down the corridor and found the chapel open, so he went in. Peace took hold of him, and he knew she would be all right, but he also knew she would never be his. Yet he was still at peace. That had happened years ago and he had not discussed it, but he wanted to know about that peace and about that chapel.

After several months of instruction I received him into the Church. Later he went into the Marines, where some of the drill instructors thought he should learn to hate, or at least to depersonalize the enemy. He couldn't. I had given him a copy of a little meditation book by Anthony Paone, called *My Daily Bread*. It was based on the *Spiritual Exercises* of Ignatius Loyola, set up for daily reading. It spoke to him. And he spoke to Christ. Every future letter or visit from him humbled me and deepened our sharing.

In one letter, he told me that on Parris Island a drill instructor had gotten angry at him for his lack of aggressiveness. I guess he didn't make "Geronimo!" sound nuclear enough when he was bayonetting a dummy. The drill instructor had jammed the butt of his rifle into his face and knocked out several of his front teeth. He had not a word of self-pity, not a word of complaint, not a request for a form to file a grievance. He had one frail comment, "I don't know how I could go through life without faith."

As I grew into the reality of what it meant to truly be a pilgrim with another man or woman in such a brutalizing world, I was drawn more and more to Thérèse of Lisieux. As much as anyone was ever a help to me, she was a friend. When she was only fourteen, she read a newspaper story of a brutal murder of a woman and child. The murderer was sentenced to death and remained hardened, unrepentant. He would have nothing to do with prayer, with confession, with a chaplain. She had seen a picture of the wounded hand of Jesus with his blood dripping onto the ground and wanted to bring people to the power of Christ's redemptive wounds. So she asked God for the soul of this murderer. In her simplicity, she asked God to give her a sign. In the newspaper account of his execution, she read that when he got up onto the scaffold, he took a crucifix and kissed the wounds of Christ. She called him her first child.

As gentle as she was, at age twenty-three and twenty-four she willingly accepted the suffering of the tuberculosis that killed her slowly, if that was Christ's will. Suffering brought redemption. We have only one life-time to live by faith.

All that can seem a very different world from the campus and the foot-ball players, but they were all part of one world. And that was where I lived.

∞

In the religion courses, I was teaching different Christian denominations, Jews, and agnostics, as well as Catholics. Many students were veterans from Korea. Evil, freedom, the nature of humanity, and God were not abstract philosophical problems to these students; they carried inside themselves intense struggles, and these struggles were our starting point.

Søren Kierkegaard often attracted such students. He had fled the hypocrisy of the established Church, the Lutheran Church, and deter-mined to be loyal only to his own experience. His courtship failed. He had no experience of an authentic human relationship—with brothers, sisters, spouse, or congregation. But he had an experience of Christ, so his world-view was Christian, though uninvolved personally in the larger Christian family. With disillusionment and alienation as their starting point, the men also responded to Jean-Paul Sartre. Sartre had no experience of Christ, no real awareness of being loved. He arrived at a system that explained and projected his own life. But all I could find in Sartre's exis-tentialism was an invitation to suicide.

I came to these classes—basically philosophy of religion classes—with an intellectual background grounded in Thomistic philosophy. But I knew I had experienced so much love in my life that it was embarrassing to deal with young men who had known little of that love and had been wounded by the ugliness and brutality of wars I had never experienced.

Many from Catholic high schools seemed to have wounds from negative experiences of religion. Much of what they had heard of the gospel had been partially denied by the circumstances in which they heard it. I wanted to help them step out of the magnet of their own intense struggle—not to a stance of intellectual dissecting but rather to a grasp of the simplicity of the ancient scriptures which could touch them personally. To do this, I could not simply teach them the way I was taught.

Many times in scripture class we all wound up on the floor. Once as we reenacted Christ's washing his disciples' feet, the young man I asked to take the role of Christ was quite shy. He agreed. When he took off his "outer garment"—his sweater—he had no T-shirt on. I was about to stop him, but the group was all so serious I decided not to. He was so strong and simple, as he quietly moved from one to another, the whole scene so simply moving. I thought that if John and Peter could look back over the years and still be humbled by remembering Jesus at their feet, perhaps these students would too.

One summer I had an evening course in the Gospels with only twelve students. I was groping for the shared experience the students needed to pull out of their own intensely private struggles and begin to be a community. I asked them whether they would be willing to preach the gospel some evening in the stand at Perry Square—the place our family used to drive on Christmas when I was a child to see the fountain lit up with colored lights. Perry Square by then had none of the beauty of my memory of Christmas lights—it was a place of drifters and alcoholics. The students agreed, tentatively, provided all of them did it. I expected only a half dozen people in the seats, maybe a few more on the edges stopping curiously. But immediately we had a crowd of seventy to one hundred people.

One of the students rose to speak on Jesus' command "Love one another as I have loved you." As he started to quote from Paul, a man in the park interrupted.

"Hey!" It was a voice that demanded attention. I looked over. The man from the crowd was tall, hairy, bearded, in T-shirt and jeans. Wrapped around him almost like ivy was a young woman who was looking at him intently with admiring eyes.

"Look, you talk about love, but I'm not sure what you mean. When I say love, this is what I mean," and he pointed at himself and his girl. "Is this love?"

I was half in a panic for the speaker, but I knew it was his project. He looked directly at the fellow and the woman. After a short pause he said, "I don't know. I can't answer your question without knowing how much you are willing to give up for her. If I knew that, I could probably give you an answer." There was no fear, no sarcasm, no disrespect. As I watched, the clinging pair didn't interrupt again. They listened, then lost themselves in the crowd. It was impressive to see a young man so settled and composed under this possible assault. And I realized that the immediacy with which he associated love and sacrifice was not the result of a few evening scripture classes.

The relationship of those early teaching years that taught me most about how to be a friend in another's journey was with one of the football players. Dan Driscoll was physically powerful. No play ever went past him. He was guileless, innocent, unassuming, but nothing came easily for him in study. While at Gannon, Dan had begun to think about the priesthood for himself, and after he had transferred to another school, he was unable to put it out of his mind.

Several times he came back to school to discuss it. Once he brought with him Thérèse of Lisieux's *Story of a Soul,* which I had given him. He read me several passages from it to help him explain his own thinking. A child of the times in which she was raised, Thérèse had felt the heroic impulse: "I feel the *vocation* of the WARRIOR, THE PRIEST, THE APOSTLE, THE DOCTOR, THE MARTYR. . . ." But active forms of heroism were beyond her. In her distress, she opened the New Testament to chapter 13 of Paul's Epistle to the Corinthians:

> . . . the Apostle explains how all the most PERFECT gifts are nothing without *LOVE*. That *Charity is the EXCELLENT WAY* that leads most surely to God.
>
> I finally had rest. . . .
>
> *I understood it was Love alone* that made the Church's members act, that if *Love* ever became extinct, apostles would not preach the Gospel and martyrs would not shed their blood. I understood that LOVE COMPRISED

ALL VOCATIONS, THAT LOVE WAS EVERYTHING, THAT IT
EMBRACED ALL TIMES AND PLACES.... IN A WORD, THAT IT WAS
ETERNAL!

Then, in the excess of my delirious joy, I cried out: O Jesus, my Love...
My *vocation*, at last I have found it . . . MY VOCATION IS LOVE!

. . . in the heart of the Church, my Mother, I shall be Love . . . . (Thérèse
Martin, *Story of a Soul* [Washington, D.C.: Institute of Carmelite Studies,
1975], p.194)

There was Dan with this huge body and this little book and the con-
viction that his vocation to love for him meant priesthood. I admired him
and his honesty, but I knew his limited intellectual ability, so I warned
him, "Dan, I don't know whether you have a call to priesthood, but I can
tell you that if you do, you'll have to work much harder than your class-
mates. You'll have to want it a great deal and be willing to face tough
rejections." That didn't bother him.

He went into the seminary. Every school year ended with his being on
probation. When it was time for subdeaconate, he was not ordained. As a
subdeacon, he would be bound to read the Divine Office every day, and
that would take time from his studies.

His bishop had given orders that no one could be ordained if he was
not at ease with Latin. The bishop invited Dan and three other candidates
in question to supper with the intention of evaluating them individually
after the meal. Dan described to me his inability to eat, and his prayer of
abandonment in which he would accept whatever came. After supper, the
bishop took him to a study, opened the breviary and asked him to read.
As he read aloud, the reading flowed. The bishop was satisfied; Dan was
amazed.

I went to New England to preach at his first Mass. Then I prayed that
he wouldn't spend his life as a football coach. When I saw him next, he
was radiant. His pastor was a bit gruff, but he wanted Dan to do a door-
to-door census of the parish. Not just Catholics, but everyone. After six
months at it, Dan told me how grateful he was that he wasn't coaching.
He liked being in homes. "That's where the action is. You have to be there
for awhile, so people know they can talk to you. Then they talk. You just

have to love God and listen and let things happen. If I ever become a pastor, I want to get someone else to do all the administration so I can be with the people."

Mass was still in Latin and Dan still stumbled. One Sunday as he was reading from an epistle of St. Paul he got so confused he had to stop and start over several times. He found comfort in thinking that Jesus was more simple than Paul, so he thought reading the Gospel would be easier. When it was just as much a problem, he wanted to pick up the book and bookstand and throw them out into the congregation.

After Mass, he didn't go to greet the people. He was too angry. He waited till the church was empty, then he went in and tried to pray. And he heard a voice saying, "Who the hell told you to be a Latin scholar; I told you I wanted you to be a priest." He was startled.

I said, "Dan, do you think what you were doing got Jesus so upset he said 'hell?'" Our eyes met and he smiled.

I went to visit him shortly before his early death, humbled by his faith and his loyalty to the vocation of Love. And grateful to Thérèse.

5

The Eucharist in a Mexican Hut

AS I CAME TO KNOW MORE AND MORE STUDENTS, I COULD SEE little purpose in a Catholic college without a challenge to a life of prayer and service, little honesty in a situation that did not help to achieve it. In the early days, many of the veterans of World War II and Korea had seen battle and returned grateful for life itself. Then retreats for large groups with powerful liturgies produced some honest contact with Christ in a living Church. Slowly the impact of the large liturgies and the docility on which they were based diminished.

At the same time, the clatter of wall-to-wall sound—the car radio, the multiple–T.V. homes, the overwhelming volume of electronic sounds—was becoming deafening. The constant battering of the senses with sounds and novelty, the constant clamor of excitement and the fireworks of the moment seemed to feed a short attention span. How, I wondered, can a person find renewal inside of himself or herself when reality is ground into hamburger to be easily digested? When reality means fast answers to quick questions? For prayer, for friendship, there needed to be spiritual growth, and the situations that make growth possible.

When a person living in such a climate comes upon some chunks of time to be shared with other people or with God, they need to learn new skills. For friendship, with people and with God, takes time. The call to holiness was not, as many thought when I first became a priest, a call only to the religious vocation. The call to holiness was for everyone.

To jolt the students out of the self-indulgence that seemed to block this deepening of life, I felt it was important that they encounter individual men and women who were seriously concerned about the interior life. I began taking a group of students committed to meditation and social service to the Trappist monastery at Gethsemani, Kentucky. There they spoke with Thomas Merton—not about his writings but about his life.

The monastery, the retreats, brought a grounding in the interior life. But I was moving beyond my earlier desire to be a Trappist. Holiness was not limited to "a monastery garden," as I once had pictured it. And holiness was not something private, between me and God.

The ancient message of Christ—go to the poor—began to reach our group in a fresh way through strong images of poor men and women in Asia, in Latin America, in Africa. I was particularly moved by the story of a young mother who came to an American relief agency seeking milk for her baby. The workers apologized—they had no milk. All they could give her was rice. The woman accepted the package, walked down the road a short way; then she sat down in the road, looked at her sagging breasts and her child, put a handful of rice into her own mouth to soften it and moisten it; then took it from her mouth and put it into the mouth of the baby.

The monastery experience quieted the inner din and brought me, and the students, into contact with a small community of men who accepted the reality of the spiritual and shared it. To learn to live this in our own lives, I believed that we needed to enter into the life of the poor in another culture, among people for whom the reality of the spiritual pervades each day.

⌒

One summer while three students and I spent time at the University of Ponce in Puerto Rico, we went to visit the mountain village of Orocovis to meet a legendary old Irish priest named Father Barry. When we arrived, about twenty people were waiting to see him for confession and to pray with him. They carried gifts of food—bananas, fruit, chickens, and eggs. They went in one at a time, and we waited till they were finished.

Father Barry seemed ancient. He was blind, and his cassock was spotted and a bit grimy. Stacks of dusty Irish newspapers lay around the room. He had a large cardboard box for eggs; as he was talking, he was feeling his way into the little bags the people had brought. With a shaking hand, he'd remove the eggs and feel his way into the box so he could deposit the eggs without breaking them.

He told us his story: As a young priest he had left his home in Ireland to come to Puerto Rico without knowing any Spanish. When he came, this poor parish had not had a pastor for years. But as soon as the people knew he was a priest they accepted him. They gathered in their own homes, sometimes crying with joy, sometimes singing with gusto. He said Mass at the parish church there for several months before he had mastered enough Spanish to preach. His first sermon in Spanish was on the passage "There has stood in the midst of you, one whom you have not known, the latch of whose sandal I am unworthy to loose."

As he spoke with the four of us in his small room, he began drifting into Spanish, forgetting us, drifting back through his life some forty years. We sat silently, dwarfed, as he preached again his first Spanish sermon. Then he said, "I have kept the eternal priesthood in Orocovis for over forty years." We asked about coming to live among the people. And he cautioned us: "Some think that all you need to get to heaven is the Bible, but no book ever gets people to heaven. People don't learn God just by reading. They need Jesus—someone who loves Jesus to speak to them, to give them the gospel, to give them the Eucharist."

At that point I started planning an extended retreat—for the students, for me—into a simpler, poorer, more reverent culture, where we would live among the people, sharing their way of life.

∞

We chose Yucatan, Mexico. With the first group of students, I drove through St. Louis, Brownsville, Mexico City, and then over the old highway and the ferries to Merida. We drove twenty-four hours a day, taking turns driving and sleeping. Our destination: a small, poor village called Sotuta, populated mostly by Mayan Indians who lived in thatched huts. With the help of a local carpenter, the students were to build a thatched hut for a widow with several children.

When we arrived in Merida we found streets decorated with flowers, monuments, huge churches—both old and modern—and large homes, one of which housed some of our students. But Merida kept us prisoners of the twentieth century.

As three of us headed south, threading our way through the narrow back roads, we seemed to be driving into the past. When the two students saw the thatched hut in which they were going to stay, they almost turned back. When someone told them that at times they had trouble with scorpions, tarantulas, and even coral snakes, they were ready to run. I asked them at least to give it a one week's try. The two of them were to come to Merida on Friday by milk train; I half expected that they would come bag and baggage—their vocation to service a thing of the past.

When I met them at the train, I was startled by the changes in them; darker from the sun, but sturdier, surer of what they were doing. The first day that they worked, they were very nervous about insects and snakes; they wore shoes and were most cautious. But the widow's children followed them everywhere, watching these creatures from another planet beginning to clear the ground and gather the wood.

A thatched hut there has a skeleton made of ironwood, which looks like bamboo but is much sturdier. A hut ordinarily has a life expectancy of seventy-five years. Most families have two huts; one for living and sleeping, one for cooking and eating. The widow's living hut was no longer stable. She had no husband to build her another, no money to afford one, and her children were too small to be of any help. But they knew the new hut would be theirs.

With wide eyes they watched the blond strangers carry stones and begin to build. As the hours and days passed, the only son, who was about four years old and completely naked, watched, but never said a word to them. In the late afternoon as they were leaving Sotuta, he said a single word that secured their vocation: "Gracias."

Several times I visited the village, occasionally overnight. I love the laughter of the children, the playfulness of the families. Each time I felt surer that the young people of Sotuta, looking forward only to life in a thatched hut, were happier than the students I taught. Even in Merida, it was not unusual to see a well-dressed woman carrying a live chicken or two on the bus, bringing home the family meal. The children seemed to respect their parents' managing of the basic needs—secure in knowing that their mother knew how to cook a chicken.

One summer, while the students were working in Sotuta and Merida, I was preparing a book for a high school religion series. Fortunately, I was invited to stay on a ranch where I would have privacy and quiet. There I saw another side of Mexico. The Santa Anna ranch was huge, including a village for the people who worked there raising bulls for the ring. There was a small convent with three sisters, a chapel where I said Mass daily, a ranch house with many bedrooms, and a pasture that extended up into the mountains, so that the bulls raised on the ranch could grow up wild, untamed, ready to do battle in the ring.

As Chacho, as his friends called the owner, described to me his bulls' successes, I couldn't understand his excitement. So I studied a bit about bullfighting and went to the ring. I was amazed at a custom I had never understood, at the excitement and splendor that took hold of all who were there. I was entering an old world of ritual that was a mystery to me. While some reservations remained, it was a new warning to me about the danger of dismissing what we do not know.

Each day I'd rise early and, after meditating, offer Mass for a group of thirty people. Each day I'd have a six-course dinner in a huge dining room, seated alone at a table large enough for sixteen captain's chairs. After dinner, I'd go horseback riding. The manager, Manuel, never let me go alone. He accompanied me the first two times; then he delegated one of the others. Four weeks later I still had not seen the whole ranch. After the ride, I'd rest and plan for more writing. Around eight o'clock I'd have a final meal that was very much like breakfast with the quiet and recollection. I was young again.

As a priest, I was treated with a deference I was unaccustomed to. The children and the villagers would run up and try to kiss my hand. One afternoon when it had been raining, I went riding. I had put on clean pants that morning, and I was trying to direct my horse between puddles and around them. The horse had more sense than I did, but in letting me be in charge, he slipped in the mud, and I was immersed in it, my clothes sopping. I wasn't hurt, but my guide was tremendously alarmed, then frightened at how Manuel would react. On our way back to the stable, we passed the children. Since I was so prestigious in their minds, they knew it was not proper to laugh, but they could hardly contain themselves. One would titter and try to hide. The others would get caught up in the tittering until there was no place to hide.

Manuel was in no way amused. His hostility was directed at the guide, and for the next few days he wouldn't let him accompany me. Along the highways in rural Mexico, if someone is killed in an accident his relatives build a memorial next to the road—a simple reminder, a request for prayer, and a warning—especially on dangerous curves of winding mountain roads, where there might be five or six memorials on top of one another. One day I told Manuel that I wanted to build a mortuary by the mud hole where I had my accident. He wasn't sure that he understood me and wasn't sure that I understood what I was saying. He looked at me intently, trying to read me. Then I smiled. He relaxed and laughed and laughed. The next day, my old guide came with me again.

Three times I drove the long trip to Mexico with the students. Once when I was in Yucatan for several weeks the priest in the parish on Cozumel was taken ill, and I flew there to take care of the liturgy. The sacristan took a few of us out in his boat to go skin diving. The first day I stayed in the boat, and watched. The next day I got a tank and went down. There I saw a world I hadn't even dreamed of: splendid corals in all forms, sizes, shapes, and colors; great schools of fish in almost endless streams of color; the sun touched everything. I glimpsed the impulse of moving from one fascination to another, forgetting everything, even the responsibility of going back.

One morning, a man in his thirties arrived at the rectory wanting to have a priest to take care of his father, who was dying. We traveled in his jeep over very rugged hillsides to the edge of the island. There was a lonely thatched hut, which seemed to me to be a piece of Africa. Inside, the only furniture was a thin hammock strung from one side of the room to the other. A thin, skeletal remnant of a man was lying in it. He was wrinkled, gray, breathing with difficulty. His wife, herself just a wisp of a human being, was gently swinging the hammock to cool and comfort him. She said nothing, but she was obviously glad at my arrival. She and her son left for a few minutes. The boy had told me his father had not received the sacrament for years, and I wanted to hear his confession. After confession, I called them back in, and they knelt there as I anointed the man. However, when I tried to give him communion, he pointed to his throat and shook his head.

The woman was on her feet almost at once; she took a small piece of cotton from a box and pointed to a glass of juice. Her husband had some throat obstruction, but if she dipped the cotton in juice and placed a small particle of the host on it, when he sucked in the juice, she knew he could receive communion. No theology; no embarrassment. She just wanted to give her husband communion before he died. I agreed readily, and she gave him communion. As soon as he received communion, she fainted. I realized she was hardly breathing, and while her son went for the doctor, I anointed her and prayed for her. She died just after her son returned. After a while, he said we ought to go back to the rectory. On the way back, I learned that he was one of ten children, but the only one who survived infancy. He loved his mother and would miss her a great deal, but he was convinced that she had gone on living for years after she was not strong enough to live simply because she did not want to die without helping her husband to make peace with God. When that happened, he knew she realized that her work was done. He didn't expect that his father would outlive her by more than a few days. The faith and love and simple reverence for the Eucharist that were brought together in that thatched hut were enormous. "The strap of her sandal I am unworthy to loose."

ထာ

Manuel was the first man I ever met who had made a Cursillo. Manuel told me that before he made a Cursillo he had gone to Mass most Sundays, though he had excused himself quite easily. If there was a sermon, he would be irritated. If it was a long sermon, he would be positively hostile, because he had so many important things to do.

Then he made a Cursillo.

He started to understand the Mass. He tried to explain it to me: the Mass is the most important thing we do. If only we could get people to understand it and enter into it, their lives would change. Since making the Cursillo eight months earlier, he had received the Eucharist every day.

When Bishop Hervas of the island of Majorca had first formed the Cursillo, he wanted it to be just that. "Cursillo" means "little course." It was to be an instruction in Christianity for adult men who were culturally Catholic but who were convinced that religion belonged to women and children. They had little adult instruction in the doctrine of Christ. The Mass was for women, not for a macho man. At first the Cursillo was not open to women, because if they became very active in it, many men would shun it. After a while, it was opened to the wives of men who had made Cursillos, many of whom couldn't understand the change that had taken place in their husbands. They, like Manuel, were brought through the Cursillo to a new glimpse of the Mass. They grew and had the means of further growth, long after the Cursillo had passed.

When I heard about the Cursillo, it was like hearing a note inside me that I couldn't forget. Some years later the Cursillo found its way north, and I was able to make one myself.

The first evening, sixty of us found ourselves on cots in an old church, not even speaking to one another. The third day we had come to listen and respect and know each other—a community, formed in small groups. A Mexican student making the Cursillo with me became homesick—so much was reminding him of his early religious life and his family. Sharing in this setting made him miss his own brothers and sisters. He lay down on his cot, his eyes closed, to hide his tears. A few men not quite ready for sleep got out a guitar and started singing. Then he wasn't alone.

As I helped in Cursillos, always experiencing people giving other people the permission to be, I grew in my awareness of the Mass. At some point, in a way that affected me profoundly, I became intensively aware that the whole canon of the Mass is addressed to God the Father. The consecration calls to mind that the night before he died, Jesus took the bread, blessed it, broke it and gave it to his disciples and said, "This is my body which will be given up for you. Do this in memory of me." In like manner the wine, "This is the cup of my blood of the new and eternal covenant. It will be shed for you and for all for the forgiveness of sins."

I had repeated these words daily for years. In having a memorial service instead of a tombstone, Jesus wanted us to memorize the magnificent statement of the sacrifice of Calvary and of the Last Supper. "Whenever you do this, remember me." He, himself, would make them real in renewal. It came home to me that I was not the celebrant speaking to the congregation; I was reminding God the Father of the events being relived. Often before, I had centered my attention on the business and professional people, the teachers and the students in the pews, and told them what Christ did—and was still doing—for each of us. But now I recognized that that was not the proper focus of my thoughts. In reading scripture, in preaching, in exhorting to prayer, I was talking to the people. But as we came to the center of the Mass, I was speaking to the Father. I was reminding him of what Jesus had done and was doing. And I was aware of him being conscious of me and of my act. Then I was bathed in the completeness of his acceptance, his providence.

From then on, after that new glimpse, I found it more and more difficult to be aware of people during the Mass. Until after the sermon, my exchange with the people was easy; for me, it was joyful. But at the heart of the Mass, I could no longer center any attention on the people. I certainly did not want them to go away. As a liturgist, I wanted to lead them into the presence of God. When we were there consciously, the minutiae of our own relationships were not important. There are several different canons for the Mass. They are to be followed precisely and used carefully. I had memorized them, so neither the book nor my bifocals required any attention. All honor and glory—and full attention—belonged to God the Father.

And if God loved his people and had infinite power, there was no need of anxiety for the bread of the day. When the celebration warranted it, he would provide even raisin bread or cake. The pressures of this season would pass—this century, twentieth or twenty-first—is so transient. All things pass. God alone remains. And he remains unconditionally loving as he was that night when in response to his will, Jesus took bread and wine, accepted a crucifixion, and entered into the fullness of his life. The Father doesn't need to be reminded of his Son's great act of love. In each

Mass—and in everything that makes a Cursillo a community and a people his people—I think of God embracing us in the light of this greatest work of love.

Over a ten-year period I visited Mexico three times. Some of our students stayed for two years. Over the years we built relationships that brought about twenty-five Mexican students to Erie to study. Most returned to live in their own country.

As I had done before going to Mexico that first summer, I still worry about people whose inner dialogue is an uproar, stilled only by some substance, by loud music and noise, or by excitement. Lassie coming home won't do any more. Hill Street blood will do it better. I worry about those who can find no renewal inside themselves. Shells of human beings that have not known friendship with other people or friendship with God. And I worry about those who dread silence, who endure it, or who think that a star is some highly paid and wildly admired human being on this planet.

Manuel had the mountains and the stars as Moses had them, but he needed someone to teach him how to pray. The students who spent a summer in Mexico building a simple hut were from Catholic homes, but they needed help to become quiet, to learn simplicity and silence, and then to learn to pray.

After those weeks in Sotuta, the world was enriched by much more than a seventy-five-year hut.

Part Two

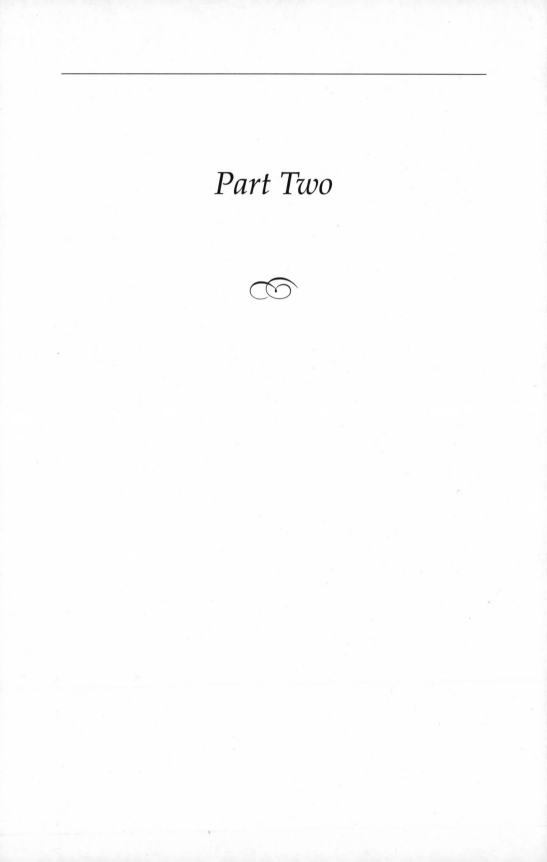

6

Suicide Park
and Oscar McGrew

∞

IN 1948, LOWER STATE STREET IN ERIE WAS A GATHERING AREA
for many broken people living in cheap rooms or out in the open. Down
near the dock was an area known as Suicide Park, which had a few abandoned storehouses where winos often gathered to drink or discuss world
affairs or eat and sleep. Below Hamot Hospital just across State Street
was the "hot plate," where city steam came close to the surface. There
people often slept at night, sometimes with a covering of newspaper to
protect them from the snow. At Sixth and State was Perry Square, with
a few monuments, a lovely fountain, and many benches. Around the
square were the bus station, a state store, City Hall, and Gannon College.
The square looked like a campus for Gannon but served also as an alter-
nate gathering place for the brethren from Suicide Park.

The treasurer's office was on the first floor of Gannon, the first office
that a visitor coming into the college would find. When one of the wan-
derers from the park would come in to ask for a handout or a meal, Gannon had no established policy. The treasurer started to refer them to me
in my basement office as a kind of joke. I couldn't handle it as a joke and
knew it would be chaotic to pass out money, so I opened a charge account
at a little restaurant on Turnpike, and if someone really needed a meal,
I'd give him a note to get one.

One day, a crippled man came to the office. He was a bit rancid with
alcohol, but most respectful. He asked me for fifty cents for a drink. That

was new. No one ever asked me for money for a drink. I knew he was honest, so I gave him the fifty cents, and I asked him to sit down for awhile.

His name was Rusty. One of his legs was short and weak. It was difficult for him to stand for any long period, but he had kept a job till eight years before. On his way to work, he would walk through the park and many times he'd help someone who asked for a quarter. Then once, when he had a two-week vacation, he decided to spend it in the park to see how the people lived there. He never went back to work. As he talked about his home and his childhood, it was obvious that he had a deep faith. Finally, he asked me to hear his confession. I told him I would be happy to hear his confession, but he would have to be completely sober. So I told him any time he would go without drinking for a week, he should come back and I would hear his confession. A week later he was back. The last drink he had was with the fifty cents I gave him.

His attitude during confession and communion was one of deep reverence. Even years later, when we were working together and became close friends and he would tease me a bit aggressively to prove we were really friends, whenever it was time for confession (about once a month), he would shift gears. God's power was so real; God was so holy; Rusty was a sinner; I was a priest; and Jesus was there with us. Like children.

Not long after he came for confession I helped Rusty get a room. He put in several job applications, one at Lord's Manufacturing, where a student in our night school was personnel manager. Rusty had put my name on the application along with a work record that included eight years of doing nothing. The manager called me and asked for an explanation, and a recommendation that I couldn't give, except to say that I thought he was sincere and I hoped he could have a chance to try. He got the job. They had to make some changes in the machine he was using to allow for his handicap. But he proved to be a very good worker.

He started to save his money. Then about twice a month we'd go out for supper at a Pizza Shop on Friday evening. He wouldn't let me touch the bill ever. We'd talk for an hour after dinner. I'd hear about his work, then about a woman he had started to date, and also about the brethren still in the park. When the woman realized he was getting too serious too soon, she told him she didn't want to go out anymore, and he was crushed. He withdrew all his money from the bank and started to drink.

The first I knew about it was when Doc Daley, a practicing alcoholic who was a friend of Rusty's, came to my office door. When I opened it, he jammed a wad of twenty dollar bills into my hands and said,

"Here, take care of it."

I asked, "Is it hot?

He said, "It sure is. It's Rusty's. I knew when he started to drink he'd fall asleep and somebody would roll him, so I stayed with him and rolled him."

Doc had only one leg and was on crutches, but he wouldn't stay. He thought that was all the explanation I needed, and he hobbled off. As soon as Rusty came to in the park and saw that the money was gone—it was $340—he went to the police station. The police picked up all the regular residents they could find in the square. One of them was Doc Daley. He told them what had happened, and that I had the money. They called and confirmed it. I went over to pick up Rusty. They let Doc out immediately, although he was picked up later that day for panhandling.

Through Rusty I got to know many of the people in the park. From him I got a rundown of their backgrounds and their behavior patterns. He went back to work, but he didn't start dating again. His major interests were tied up with his old friends, his work, and me. If I helped someone that Rusty thought wasn't sincere, he would be really angry, and he had a rugged temper. He'd never learn from me who came for help, because I thought it was a private matter for each person I dealt with. But when he heard it from others, he was angry that I hadn't consulted him— he was the expert—and worried that since I would never get over being naive, I would be used the rest of my life.

He asked me once whether I would help Doc Daley make a pledge to give up alcohol. I told him I'd be glad to help if Doc wanted, but I insisted that Doc would have to be sober to take the pledge. We had AA meetings at the college, and I had gotten to know a number of the men and women who came. I knew a pledge wouldn't solve Doc's problems. Even if he kept it, he would simply be putting the plug in the jug. There was much else to deal with if he was going to become sober.

One day, Rusty came to the office with a high-priced smile. Doc had been hit by a car when he was crossing the street. I couldn't understand his happiness till he explained, "He's a patient at Hamot Hospital, and now he'll have to get sober." I went down to see him. Three days later I helped him make a six-month pledge, which he kept. He wouldn't renew it though, and started to drink again.

∽

The prison was only a block from the college. Occasionally Rusty would tell me about an inmate who wanted to see me. Gradually I began to be at home in the prison, and when the cathedral rector asked me to relieve his assistant as chaplain, I agreed. I would visit all the ranges at least once a week, and was on call anytime.

As I came to know more prisoners in one-on-one encounters, over and over the same question came up: How could there be a loving God at the center of so much suffering? If God loves me, why doesn't he answer my prayer?

Slowly I realized what "prayer" meant. One man told me he had carried on a string of robberies for three years. When I asked him about prayer, he said, to be honest, the only time he prayed was when he was in danger of being caught. That's making God an accessory to the crime! When I asked another whether he prayed, he said, "Only when I'm in real trouble." I told him, "If I were God and loved you, I'd keep you in trouble all the time so you would talk to me."

Each Christmas Day I celebrated Mass at the prison. I would usually have one or two Masses elsewhere on Christmas; then I'd come back to spend the afternoon and evening in the prison. The connecting of suffering with love was the point of entry to Christ for these men, but the obstacles to that message demanded some new ways of speaking with them about the basic Christian belief that starts with reality: What is God telling me about why I am here at this moment? I began to start my Christmas sermon with this thought: "This is Christmas. It's a beautiful feast. Let's all thank God for being here in jail." Often we would talk about why one would be grateful to God for being in prison on Christmas. I had to find a language to speak of God to men behind iron doors, where rage and helplessness focused on one religious notion: "If you are Son of God, save yourself and us." A language that connected love with discipline:

Suppose when you were a boy you went out into the yard and found an ugly, mangy, flea-bitten mutt. You feel sorry for it, and bring it home. Your father meets you at the door and says, "Get that thing out of here." Right away, you say,

"Dad, can I have him? I'll take care of him."

"No, you won't. You'll be interested for one afternoon. Then your mother will have to take care of him. She'll be feeding him and cleaning up after him. I know you."

Now your Dad has one weak spot. He loves you. It's hard to understand why, but he loves you. So he agrees, but he's clear:

"The first time I find your mother having to clean up after him, we're getting rid of him."

You're glad. You take him downstairs and give him a bath. He thinks you're trying to drown him. He messes on the floor. You rub his nose in it and put him out. If you come home from school and your little sister has him up on the couch petting him, you make a club out of newspaper and hit him with it. If that dog could think, he'd figure that if it weren't for you, he'd have a happy home. And you are the one most concerned about him.

A long time ago, when you and I were scrawny mutts morally, Jesus said to his heavenly Father,

"Can I have him?"

And God looked at you and said, "That one? I wouldn't ask a decent human being to live with him, and you want to bring him to heaven?"

But Jesus prayed and God the Father has one weak spot . . . he loves Jesus. So he gave you to Jesus. But Jesus has to get you ready for heaven. He bathes you in the water to which his word gives life, and he is strict with you because he loves you.

Whenever I preach it, I listen. I'm embarrassed to say "you" as though it doesn't include me. But if I say "we," then people can hide in global anonymity and think that Christ is using a net to catch a whole school when he is really interested in each one. For the minute, he is forgetting the ninety-nine. It is you I seek.

∞

Often when a man is first in prison, he's frantic about getting the right lawyer or bondsman, and he's certain the world can't go on without him. At least, he feels he owes it to others to get out soon, because on visiting day the place will be crowded with his visitors. When it becomes clear that he can't get out, and when after two weeks even his wife can't come because one of the children is sick, he begins to wilt. He might even surrender. When I see that he has surrendered and is at peace, I worry about his losing it as soon as he's close to parole. Somehow, it seems that if there's nothing he can do, he's at peace. The moment he thinks he can do something, he often forgets God, God's power, the need of trust, and his peace passes as though his friendship with God were a passing summer romance on shipboard.

But one of the prisoners, named Phil, wasn't like that. He took things easily. After he got out, he wanted to help a friend he had met in prison. The friend was eligible for release if he could find a job. Phil wasn't able to find a steady job for him, but he got two or three painting contracts and the parole officer agreed to his friend's release. By then, Phil had a car and he let his buddy use it to transport equipment from job to job.

The buddy used the car for a robbery and took off. When the car was found, some of the stolen goods were still in it. Phil was picked up immediately and put back in prison. On the range others told him he ought to send for me. After a bit of thinking, he said "I could call for Father, and I know he'd come. But I know what he'd say: 'If you were doing your best and this is what happened, it must be what God wanted.'" He said after he figured that out, he realized he hadn't listened to what he thought I would say. So suddenly he arrived himself at the conclusion, "God must want me in jail." Then he asked, "I wonder why?" And he concluded it must be for the good of the others on the range. By the time I arrived on Saturday, he had three of them wanting to talk to me very seriously.

I offered to go to the trial as a witness, because I knew the two people and the circumstances. The defense attorney put me on the stand and asked questions discreetly enough that it seemed to me the issue was settled. But in summation, he shifted the whole case to me, and pointing at me, he asked, "Did you ever see a sweeter, more gentle man of the cloth?" The result was a hung jury. I was convinced that any serious juryman would figure that I was a babe in the woods, gullible in the extreme, and therefore easily manipulated by a man with Phil's background. At the same time, there was nothing in Phil's track record to make it likely that he would try to help another person just from the goodness of his heart. For Phil, it meant another three months in jail. In money, counting salary he lost and attorney's fees for two trials, it cost him several thousand dollars. Phil never flinched in his trust or his joy. He wasn't the least bit fanatic, but neither was he the least bit bitter. He was acquitted in the second trial, and hasn't been in legal trouble since.

During the time I was prison chaplain, the local paper carried reports almost monthly of robberies in the churches of Erie, but none of them took place in Catholic churches. When I was on my way to the county prison, I'd often go through the courthouse. The detectives sometimes kidded me about the robberies. They said it was probably an Irish Catholic letting his prejudice interfere with his livelihood. When the thief was caught, he wasn't a Catholic at all. They had failed in guessing his *modus operandi*.

I saw him in jail twice before he wanted to talk. Then he explained to me that he had broken into three different Catholic churches, but each time he did, he felt something different. It was a presence he hadn't experienced elsewhere. He just hadn't been able to take anything while he was there. He asked whether I could explain it. I asked him whether he had ever heard of the Blessed Sacrament. He hadn't. I described the Last Supper. Jesus was leaving his friends, wanted to leave them something to remember him by, and wanted to be with them in the pressures ahead. He took bread, blessed it, broke it, said "This is my body, to be broken for you." He took the cup of wine, blessed it, and said "This is the chalice of my blood to be shed for you."

"We believe that the bread was no longer simply bread. It was the body of Christ—a real presence. After Mass, any of the consecrated hosts are stored in the tabernacle. When you go into a Catholic church, that little sanctuary light that is burning gives testimony to the real presence."

He was so deep in thought, I didn't say any more. He couldn't believe that he could believe it. He had never imagined that God could give such a gift. He started instructions, but in court he pleaded guilty, so he wasn't in the county prison long enough to finish his instructions. He finished them at the Western Penitentiary.

One very warm summer evening I was doing some counseling, but the office was so warm the two of us went outside and were sitting on a kind of abutment that separated the lawn from the sidewalk. We were finishing up because I had another engagement when one of the "knights of the road" came along asking whether we knew Father Peterson. I acknowledged that I did, and we started to talk. Someone had told him I could help him get something to eat. I went in and wrote a note for him, then apologized that I couldn't stay longer, but suggested that we walk together since we were going in the same direction. As he stepped out into the street, I had to pull him back because he almost stepped into the path of an oncoming car. He explained that when he had jumped off the freight train, he had hurt his neck and could turn it in only one direction—and even that was with much pain. He refused to go to the hospital. They would want him to go into traction, and that was no way to spend the hottest part of the summer. His mind was made up to get a meal and catch the next train—and he meant "catch." I told him that was dangerous, but he would not be dissuaded. So I asked him if I could pray for him. I put my hands on his head and asked Jesus for healing and for protection as he traveled. He thanked me with a most beautiful smile. Then the two of us went our separate ways.

A week later, I was sitting on the abutment again, counseling, and along came the man with the beautiful smile with someone else in tow. When he saw me, he pointed me out to the other man, "Here, this is the man I told you about. Let's ask him."

Then he said, "Father, this guy has some real bad trouble with his eyes. It's hard for him on the road, and he wants you to pray for him." Then he told me what happened when he left me the week before. He said, "When I left you, my whole neck felt warm. I turned it all the way to the right and it didn't hurt at all. Then I turned it to the left and expected I would have a sharp pain all the way up the back of my head. There was no pain at all. I've had no trouble with it since. I know if I went to a hospital and told them about it, they'd say there was nothing wrong in the first place, but I know that's not so. God healed me. I know it, and I thanked him." He decided not to leave town. For a while at least his "headquarters" was in Griswald Plaza near the train station. He sent or brought any number of people to me. I'd pray with them and talk with them.

With the help of Rusty and a number of others, I came to know most of the really troubled people in downtown Erie. The Anchor Inn was a pretty wild bar with rooms on the second floor, where very desperate people eked out an existence from check to check. There and at several other places, the residents could get drinks on a bar bill that meant a good deal of each check was mortgaged before it came. So many of the residents of the cheap rooming houses and cheap hotels were sick and almost abandoned. Almost everyone looked at them as though they were an intrusion. The world made it clear that it would be well served if they just got lost.

At first I was embarrassed by their friendship. If I were walking through the park with a student or a businessman and someone drunk came toward me with the delight of finding someone who cared for him—and possibly a meal—I would squirm and somehow make an apology for such behavior.

As they came to my college office, just for survival I had to try to impose rules. I moved to a series of offices that were in marginal buildings acquired to be taken down as Gannon expanded—part of the college, but with an opening to the plains. At first my phone was an extension of the college switchboard, which Doctor Wehrle, the president, handled from his room during part of each weekend. My involvements spread so much that he asked me to get a phone of my own. When I told him it had arrived, he came down personally to my office and pulled the extension cord right out of the wall so he could get some rest.

If ever a hat or coat was missing, I was a suspect—at least because of my friends. One evening, I stopped at a fraternity party to which I had been invited by a student. It was obvious that most of the students didn't want me there. The lights were a bit dim. They were two-by-two in the mood for some necking. They expected me to realize that I didn't belong and make a graceful exit, but I decided not to. I made myself at home, to their utter discomfort. Jokingly at first, they wondered if I weren't needed elsewhere. Then their comments became more than a bit barbed. I left after about an hour, but I was vividly aware that for the first time in years,

I had been in a situation where I knew I was not wanted. I was humbled again as I always am when I realize the love that has surrounded me all my life, but I had a whole new sense of loneliness of the unwanted, the sick, the aged, and the broken.

Sooner or later many of them assume—with some validity—that "anyone who helps me has some angle." He needs the income from the bar. He wants sex. He enjoys power over others. A parolee will find the man who offered him a job exploiting him, threatening him. It has amazed me how many people on the road are used for sex. Occasionally, one of the winos from the park would have things easy for awhile with the help of some business or professional woman. Those who knew about it were quite casual and excusing. Their interpretation was simple. "He's her jocker." At Griswald Plaza, a youngster who needed money for partying or for survival could wait for a homosexual to pick him up and help him out—at a price.

At the jail one evening, I was talking to a man who had been on the road a long time. He was black. He had often been rejected because of his color and poverty. He was not a Catholic, but was opening his life in a tremendous lament for the human condition. There was such ugliness in what people had done to him and in what he had done to people. He had been involved in all kinds of perverted sexual orgies with husband and wives together, kinkiness with men and women who wanted the world to accept them as upstanding and wholesome. When I asked him what he regarded as the greatest guilt on his part, he said that the distortions in sex with whites didn't bother him at all. "Whitey" always projected himself as high and mighty. So when he was invited to any kind of sexual acts, he enjoyed the opportunity of rubbing "whitey's" nose in his own filth. Stealing from people whose own thefts had been craftier and undetected didn't bother him. Looking over all the years, what he regretted most was the good things he could have done that he did not do.

∞

When I first started to have Mass at the prison, the only place large enough for a gathering was the basement shower room. We had a few primitive benches and an equally primitive portable altar on which I offered Mass in Latin with my back to the prisoners. Early on Sunday morning, I would pick up two Gannon freshmen and take them with me to have a seven o'clock Mass at the prison. During the sermon and the cleanup afterward, the students were wide awake. As we left I had many questions to answer. Almost always, they would describe one or another man and ask why he was in prison. Usually, I'd pass over that particular question. But once, a student said,

"That guy that was sitting next to me seems like a real nice guy. What's he in for?" This time, I answered.

"Murder."

He was astonished. "He doesn't look like a murderer."

So I asked, "What does 'a murderer' look like?"

Oscar McGrew had been sentenced to death for murder before I met him. He seemed to me an honest man, a little bit slow, but very respectful. He had killed his own son. He was in anguish about his guilt, his family, his wife, his other son. He had been refused a new trial, but his attorney was working to get a pardon from the governor. The warden was much in favor of it. Oscar, who had been in prison some time, was a model prisoner. When I met him first, he had a Bible, which he couldn't understand, so I gave him a child's catechism, which he read earnestly. We discussed it often; he hadn't thought much about God's love and forgiveness. He had been bleak for months in the notion that God would never forgive a man for killing his own child. He had not even imagined that could happen. It was an affront to God.

Here was a childlike faith—God was real, and God was good. He had only to see that no act of his, no matter how ugly, could block God's love for him. God loved him as he had loved his own children when he wasn't monkeying around with drugs and when he was his real self. When he finally accepted that Christ's death was enough reason for God to forgive him and when he accepted God's forgiveness, the bleakness lifted. The winter was over and past. But he told me how many of his buddies were living the same way he had been. No one ever spoke to them about anything important, so they just partied all the time. If he got a pardon, he wanted to spend the rest of his life helping people who had messed up their lives as he had.

I heard a minister tell him one time that he should keep up his hope even if he didn't hear any good news because often a pardon came at the last minute, as it had to the good thief. He answered, "Oh, I wouldn't put my hope in something like that. Hope is in God. The good thief had his prayer answered on the cross, but he asked for what God wanted him to have."

He told me later that he had stopped praying for his pardon. "This is how I figure it. Now that I know that God loves me, I know that if he doesn't think I'm ready, the pardon will come. If the pardon doesn't come, it must be that God thinks I'm ready. If God wants me and thinks I'm ready, there would be something wrong with me to hold back from God." That was almost three months before he was to be executed.

The last thing he gave me before he left the county prison to go to Rockview for his execution was the catechism that had freed him. He asked me to give it to his wife and to ask her to be sure to teach their other son what it said.

The pardon didn't come. I didn't go to Rockview with him, but the local paper carried an account of the execution. Oscar was calm. He needed no help to get to the hall or to the electric chair. The executioner, who was doing his job for the first time, was quite nervous, so Oscar fastened the bands to his own legs. Then he sat back in the chair and waited. Then came that tremendous jolt of electricity. Then a lesser jolt to be sure. Oscar thought that if God thought he was ready, there would be something wrong with him to hold back from God.

Physically, Oscar was not especially attractive. In fact, he appeared a bit obnoxious. He was slow mentally, and his attorney tried to use that in his defense. I am confident, though, that if he had been handsome and winsome, no jury would have recommended the death sentence whatever else was involved; the real crime that brought about his death was that he "looked like a murderer."

Years later, one summer evening, I was walking along a corridor in the college dorm where I was living at the time. We had an Upward Bound program for helping high school students who were in danger of flunking out. On one door was the card—Oscar McGrew. I was astonished, but I knocked and a young man came to the door. It was Oscar's son. He knew his father had been executed, but that was all. We spent a couple of hours while I explained to him what I knew of his father. He asked many questions, thought many thoughts, and realized that his father was a great man who regretted having failed him but who hoped for great things from him.

Those hours with Oscar's son were a time when the world stopped. Possibly God took care of it without the two of us.

∞

The first time I talked to a young man who was back at the county prison for a retrial after a stay at the Allegheny Workhouse, he told me that he had been raped repeatedly. What bothered him most was that he was start-ing to enjoy it. He knew there was no way to avoid it there. He just hoped that he wasn't becoming a lifelong homosexual. Within six weeks, I talked to three others who had had the same experience there. I went to the Erie County judges individually to ask them not to send any more there. Try-ing to mollify me, they warned that prisoners often lie and manipulate. But within a few months the judges adopted a policy about not sending prisoners to the workhouse. Not long afterward, it was closed.

But the problem wasn't limited to the workhouse; it goes on and on. A young man who is physically attractive in the least goes into the West-ern Penitentiary or the Eastern as available meat. He can't turn to any-one in authority when he is threatened. That would make him a snitch. His life would be unlivable. Any old-timer would advise him, "You have to stand on your own. Get a club—a stick. The first time anyone tries any-thing, try to tear him apart even if you get beat up. When that happens two or three times, they'll let you alone." If he lets people push him around, he's a punk.

Anytime I read about a candidate for District Attorney or judge run-ning on a law-and-order ticket, I wonder what "law" and what "order"—overloaded prisons, wardens and superintendents no longer able to see individual inmates even for a short conversation, dealing with structures and unions. With two men in cells built for one, without a budget for pro-grams that are really needed, the prison is a zoo. When a law-and-order judge sends a man to a prison where he is at the mercy of an unmerciful population, there is no order. The broken people are more broken.

Survival means being a hard guy and a bad guy and forgetting the outside. The inmate who is worried about not having a letter from his wife or his girl; the man who is afraid his wife can't get a job or get mother's assistance is told by others, "Forget it. If she were in here and you were out there, you'd be running around. If you worry every time you don't get a letter, you'll have a breakdown. Nobody can do hard time like that very long." As part of his survival, he says, "I don't care. I don't care. I don't care." At first, it's a lie. He does care. But to survive, he kills part of himself. The defenses an inmate builds up to protect himself in jail go out of prison with him. They are attitudes that get him in trouble with the law almost immediately, and he brings them back to jail when he comes. "I can play their game. I've done it before." The development of that attitude means that a term in jail is not nearly the deterrent it seemed earlier. Sometimes it's even an invitation—a kind of refuge from the uncertainty of life on the streets, especially in winter.

But considering prison as a game is an avenue to regarding all life situations as games; minuets with their own choreography, their own rules of rehearsal. Eventually no one is in touch with anyone—no love, no communion, no real contact with people or with God.

Breaking into the loneliness of that cycle is an awesome vocation. The Lord asks the prophet, "Do you think these bones can walk around?" Not unless the Spirit enters in and stirs them.

With the Spirit though, I know those bones will walk around.

7

Now—And the Hour
of Our Death

IN JUNE 1950, MY MOTHER HAD A SEVERE HEART ATTACK. DAD RETIRED
to care for her. They had several beautiful years together at home, but in
1955 she had another attack. It was clear to us all that she did not have
long to live.

One evening, after she had been anointed, I stopped to see her. I
brought her communion myself only once, and that time she had been so
full of happiness that I was afraid she would have another heart attack.
So I asked a priest from her parish to bring her communion. This evening,
I was on the bed beside her and we were alone. For the first time since it
happened, she spoke of our visit in the hospital when Tom was ten years
old. She said how happy she was that I had listened to God and helped
her to listen to him. Then she spoke for a while about how good God is,
how kind it was that she had not only the ten years she asked for but all
the others too. And now "Tom is all raised."

I didn't realize it at the time, but Mom, who never wanted anything for
herself, had gotten a new dress when Tom was married. That was proper.
She was the mother of the groom. But after the wedding, she put the
dress in a garment bag and stored it away so she could be laid out in it.
She thought her work was done.

Dad had retired so he could take care of her. Physically, their world
became very small. Each time one of us visited them, we all knew the
greatness of love that centered there. Then in 1955 on July 29, the feast

of St. Martha, Mom died. She and Dad had spent the day together. Toward evening, Mom knelt by her bed and said the rosary. Then she got up and fell across the bed. Her work was done.

Among her things, we found a note she must have written several months before when she was having difficulty with pain and weakness:

> Dear Con and Family,
>
> I can't bear to say good-bye, but I guess it is God's will. Please don't cry for me. Only be good. You know that is all I wanted from any of you. But no one ever had more love and kindness than I did from everyone. Be good to your wives and children and Dad because he was so good to me. I love all of you. Please keep in touch with Jim and Marie, and will all of you do what you can for Minnie, Will and Hattie, and Ora.

Then because Dad could never find keys and insurance policies, she made a list of where to look for things and told us where to find the new dress she had bought for Tom's wedding.

Dad was hardly able to function. I went with him to the funeral parlor. There were a number of caskets in a large room with neat little metal signs that said $2,000, $1,800, $1,500—all very neat and uncommercial. The price was for the specific coffin with all the service included. I asked, "Haven't you any cheaper?"

The attendant answered, "Yes, but they are over there," and he pointed.

I said, "Let's go over there." One of them in grey cloth said $850. I asked, "Is that the cheapest you have?"

He said it was, and I told him we'd take it. Dad looked at me inquiringly and asked,

"Are you sure?"

"Yes, I'm sure. Mom wouldn't want to put any money in the ground."

The first funeral I can remember was that of my Uncle Con. He was buried at St. Teresa's in Union City. The vestments were black; the Mass and the singing were in Latin. My clearest image is of the burial at the cemetery. The wind was biting. Old Father Ring was bundled up in a heavy hat, coat, and boots. Snow was covering them and him and us. Dad and Cassie and Margaret and the O'Neill girls were crying. We prayed quickly and left.

As a priest, I came to be involved as celebrant and preacher in all the family funerals. Slowly I began to experience the Communion of Saints as more than a phrase repeated in the *Credo*. I began to experience a bond with those who had died. With each uncle or aunt who was buried, I found it a joy to reflect on the love that had been in his or her life. To say even a few words about the love with which each one loved was not easy. I felt so much gratitude to God for his providence in dealing with each one, and for making each of them part of his providence in dealing with us.

But I couldn't preach when Mom died. I would have embarrassed everyone there, myself included. Archbishop Gannon presided at Mom's funeral, but Father Cooper preached. The Gospel he read was John's account of the sadness of Martha and Mary at the death of their brother Lazarus. Martha said to Jesus, "If you had been here, my brother would not have died." I knew that Martha was more aggressive than Mom. Mom would never have said that to Jesus. But Jesus would have said to her, "I am the resurrection. If anyone believes in me, even though he dies, he will live, and whoever lives and believes in me will never die."

After the reading, Father Cooper began, "Mrs. Peterson was a woman who never let the passing ups and downs of this world interfere with what was really important in life." I was amazed that he knew her so well and could focus so immediately on her splendor. God was important. Dad was important. We were important. People were important. New coats were not; neither were new cars, nor second cars, nor big splashes, nor parades.

The parishioners who had been strangers to her when she came to the parish years ago, and at first seemed threatening, came in great numbers. And all of us were very little. Except for the love that was there, nothing involved could make a splash. The faith there was the rock on which to stand.

The loneliness lapped around the edges, and we leaned on each other.

I had come to love to preach at funerals. With people jolted from their being-in-control, disappointed in God, angry at him, it is such a moment for the spirit to move. Preaching the word is an important part of priesthood, but my sense of preaching began to shift and change—not just style or technique, but how I was being God's instrument at this moment.

Many times since I was young I had listened to Bishop Gannon's preaching—and he was effective. Every time he spoke to us I held on to every word. He was high style. When he told me I could not go to the Trappists but would preach to the sisters in Erie, he also told me he wanted my sermons to be *written out.* I knew the problem in this.

The old pastor at one of the churches where I helped out initially was certain that all problems could be solved if people would only do things the way he understood they should be done. His one great desire was to build a new church as a more fitting shrine of the Sacred Heart than the little brick building called Sacred Heart Church.

One morning as I started breakfast in the rectory, the loudspeaker from the church was on. When he began to preach, the housekeeper heard only one sentence when she said, "Don't tell me it's time for that dumb thing again. I never liked it anyhow." In the lectionary, we had the same fifty-two Gospels every year—and he had the same fifty-two sermons.

The bishop told me he wanted my sermons to be written out; he never said I should read every one as I wrote it. I could not simply read what I had written. Preaching was like the one-on-one encounters I was having with so many different men and women. What I saw in each one, what I said to and shared with a suffering, or doubting, or confused man or woman could turn this person away for good. One evening, as I was preaching a retreat to a group of nurses, I knew by the end of the first session that two of them were dating married men and didn't want to break up. For a true encounter to occur, I needed to look into their eyes as much when speaking to three, or ten people, or a whole congregation, as when sitting with one alone.

I realized I was growing in a manner of preaching that was distinct from the old high style of Bishop Gannon.

∽

During the year after Mom died, I went up home each day after I was finished teaching. Sometimes it was in time for the 11:00 o'clock news, sometimes it was after midnight. Even when it was late, Dad would be waiting up. He was so lonely; I couldn't stand having him there alone all night. He'd ask, "Do you really want to come? Wouldn't you get more rest staying there?" And I'd tell him it was good to get away sometimes. We became closer friends than we had ever been. Gradually he became able to speak of Mom easily, and then of the grandchildren. One day Jack's daughter, Cathie, told him she thought Gramma had been dead long enough and we ought to go and get her. And he was broken. He'd keep toys and candy for the grandchildren as Minnie had for us. One day he asked them whether they wanted some ice cream. Someone asked, "What kind?" And he refused to give them any. Any one knows that ice cream is ice cream. To be fussy is not to be deserving.

Often I'd take him with me when I went to preach or teach. The old sisters at Titusville enjoyed his coming, his humor. It seemed almost that I was just the driver. Every time we went through Union City, he'd point out the chair factory he had helped build. And I'd hear about his best dog and some of his escapades. And about Mom. Quietly, he said, "No man has ever been loved as I have been loved, physically and spiritually."

When we went to get a headstone for Mom's grave, there were some double and some single. I said that we wanted a very simple one, and that it should be single. Dad knew that I was saying possibly in years ahead, he would want to remarry. That was the farthest thing from his mind. Several years later, he went out to dinner a few times with a very fine woman, but he couldn't feel right about it. And that was that. I suggested a Golden Age Club to him. He dismissed the idea immediately because it was for old people. Then I read about a program the club was having where an actor he had admired in minstrel shows was going to speak. He went, not for the club but for the actor. In six months, he was president of the club, where he found new, if secondary, joy in life.

∞

In my growing number of dealings with the poor, the alcoholics, and the troubled, I cared for several of them in dying. Sometimes I presided at their funerals. I remember two at St. Peter's Cathedral. The sanctuary was large. The huge church was almost empty. There were a few pallbearers that had known the dead man; they came with much shyness, yielding to me as I pressed them into service. Preaching is too large a word for what we shared there. At least someone cared.

One evening just before nine o'clock I had a call from the prison that one of the inmates had collapsed and had asked for a priest. I went over immediately. The guard took me to Range 1. At the other end of the range, I saw a man lying on the floor with a blanket over the lower part of his body. As I was going along the cells in the range, I heard one man say that the sick person used to make fifty thousand dollars a year before he started to drink. That income was rare then in Erie. When I came up to him, I knelt and called him by the name they had given me at the office. He opened his eyes, and said feebly, "Father, I think if I were in Timbucktoo and needed you, you'd come." I didn't know him. He didn't know me. I was a priest.

The only light came from a naked bulb burning outside the range, so that a shadowy latchwork of bars covered the two of us. His beard was several days old. It was smeared with mucus. He knew he was near death and was ready for confession. I never realized before how much more the courage of confession touches the future than the past. He was breathing with difficulty, but he was obviously at peace. As he finished, I asked him to pray with me a prayer for mercy. "My Jesus, mercy." Then I gave him absolution. And I was at peace. Through the ugly teeth, the beard, the mucus, what I could see was the face of Christ. Then the medics arrived and I left.

Altogether it had taken less than an hour. But everything else seemed little and small and more temporal than I remembered it. Whatever could I say? "Father, save me from this hour." No. This is why I have come to this hour. "Father, glorify your name."

∽

Bishop Gannon's mink and pages and splendor bothered me a little, but only a little. He was aware of the poor and moved splendidly for the care of orphans, the education of the children of poor families, and the care of the elderly. He was leading the children and grandchildren of immigrants out of the ghetto.

But as I taught more and more of the women studying to be sisters, serious problems became visible to me. Most of the sisters didn't drive. Many were stationed under pastors who were entrenched in minor dictatorships. For some, their only opportunity for confession was to the pastor of the church in which they were stationed. When I spoke with the bishop about it, he told me I was young and had much to learn. He didn't want to upset the sisters. As they had no real problems that required spiritual direction, the proper course was to minimize any problems they had. He never knew—or knew of—a sister who committed a mortal sin. Nothing I said could dislodge the bishop's views.

But he left me free to relate humanly to the sisters and to help lead them out of old mental patterns. I would walk out of his office free to do just about anything I wanted—anything that didn't cost the diocese money. Increasingly I realized I could go to the bishop only about problems for which I had a solution. If it were out of my competence to handle, he would belittle the problem and belittle me.

Slowly I was stretching the old, strictly defined roles of the parish priest and the college theology teacher, in response to the pain I was seeing in people pushed to the edges of our society. But they needed help beyond what I could give. A number of times I tried to move the bishop— rarely to any avail and often with much pain. Problems—people—continued to bleed. That was hard to handle.

In the months following Mom's death, I faced a conflict with Bishop Gannon. An issue arose that brought me face to face with the use of authority to exercise personal control.

The president of the college, like many a local pastor, ran a one-man operation. When evaluators questioned his method of administration, the president dismissed it lightly. I called a meeting of the priests on the faculty—a new role for me. At thirty-one, I was the youngest and in many ways the meekest one there. But no one else would act. So I did. We sent a letter to the bishop. We were challenging the leadership of the college president in a day when loyalty to the priesthood was interpreted as personal loyalty to the authority in charge.

We did not rebel. We would abide by his decision. When the lay faculty representative visited him with a similar protest, the bishop told him that the priests had not objected, because they were "loyal." Our letter was lying open on his desk.

A day later the president resigned for reasons of health. Then followed the changes necessary to save the college.

⊂⊃

The summer after Mom died, I was on my way to Notre Dame with another priest, Father Tom Miller. There was little traffic on the Ohio Turnpike, but a motorcycle that was coming toward us somehow went out of control. The driver flew up into the air as lightly and helplessly as a rag doll. He seemed to land on his face, but he rolled over and lay still. I stopped the car and we crossed the double highway. Tom moved down the road to turn any traffic into the outside lane. I went up to the young man, knelt down by the side of him, sensed his breathing. One side of his forehead seemed crushed and bloody. His other eye was closed, but there was blood running into the hollow area around it. I supported his head with my hand, lifting it ever so little.

"Can you hear me?"

Without any inflection, he said, "Yes."

"Have you ever been baptized?"

"Yes."

"Are you Catholic?"

"No."

"Would you like to pray?"

"I don't know how."

"Shall I help you?"

"Please."

"Just repeat after me—with words or in your heart: 'Jesus, I believe in you. I hope in you. I ask pardon for all my sins. I accept my pain, even my death, in union with your own pain on the cross. My Jesus mercy. My Jesus mercy.'"

A few words at a time. He repeated them. Clearly at first. Then more slowly. Then he lapsed into unconsciousness. There, with his young life running out over his face, he learned to pray. Gloves. Boots. Leather jacket. Swarthy complexion. Enough consciousness to learn. Childlike, wanting to learn to pray. No one had ever taught him.

As I prayed with him and for him, the cars began to whiz past us, speeding on their important ways. After a while, an ambulance came. We crossed the road again, got into the car, and went on quietly. "Let's say a rosary." What else? "Pray for us sinners now and at the hour of our death." Us sinners. That's who we are. That's what we have in common. Now and the hour of our death are always coming closer. The exact time we don't know. It's rare that close friends die at exactly the same time. Rare that husband and wife die at exactly the same time. But even in the loneliness that follows the separation of death, it is no small thing to have helped a person get ready for heaven. There on the highway we had a moment of communion.

As we drove away, the awareness of separation was painful. In all that was unfolding in the ministries that occupied my life, I knew that I would find neither comfort nor surprise in coincidence. A bird doesn't fall from heaven apart from the will of God. Neither does a driver fall from a motorcycle.

But then, no given day has merely some given jobs. God—people—an opportunity to serve them in prayer and friendship. Here was a young man, with a strong body, and apparently a good mind, rushing somewhere. Only: "I don't know how to pray ... I don't know how to pray." When we finished the rosary, we were just quiet. Everything irrelevant seemed irrelevant.

☙

Notre Dame that summer was splendid. The great gold dome of the administration building broadcast the sun in a statement that all was well. Sacred Heart Church was reverent, comfortable, a fit place to pray. That was the summer I found the peace of the Lourdes Grotto. Young Dr. Tom Dooley found that his heart was made peaceful there. It called him back in a kind of nostalgia, akin to what I experience when I think of the chapel at Paca Street.

I planned to go to a Benedictine Monastery in Wisconsin for retreat as soon as I left Notre Dame. Early that morning I offered Mass at Sacred Heart Church. It was July 29, the feast of St. Martha and the first anniversary of Mom's death. I was driving alone through Chicago with nothing to distract me from my memories—and my loneliness. There were a number of people on the sidewalks, but they didn't seem to have much energy, distant from one another and from life. As if no one had taught them to pray. I was feeling deeply depressed. The *Weltschmertz*, the sadness of the human condition, and my near helplessness to do anything about it seemed like too much to carry. I wanted to pray and to be with the Blessed Sacrament.

I noticed a church that had something about it that seemed Catholic, but in Chicago most of the churches were locked during the day. Even though it seemed pointless, I stopped and went over. Surprisingly, the church was unlocked. For the first time in my life, I was in a church dedicated to St. Gertrude—on the first anniversary of the death of Gertrude Ward Peterson. I was embarrassed by my discouragement and more than grateful to Jesus for the noncoincidental way in which he continued to lay out my life. After a time of very quiet, wordless prayer, I got up to leave. As I did, I noticed an altar dedicated to St. Gertrude. I went over and knelt down to pray. When I looked up, on the wall surrounding a statue was an inscription: "Confidence is the key that opens the treasury of God's graces. Saint Gertrude." The message was clear, complete. I don't know why—when I believe in the Communion of Saints—it should surprise me so, but it always does. And I went on my way glad.

In a phone call a bit later, I learned that I had a new niece, born that same day to Tom, my youngest brother, and Jean, his wife. They called her Gertrude and all of us were glad—especially Dad.

∽

In 1960 Dad died on March 19, the feast of St. Joseph. The first Mass I offered for him was the Mass of St. Joseph, his patron saint, patron of a happy death. By then the realization of the bond with those who have died—this communion we shared—was not new to me, but it was still surprising. His body was laid to rest in the cheapest coffin we could find. All that was best in him was beyond the power of the earth to contain.

In a few months that other remnant, the family home on Pine Avenue, was sold. As I visited it the last few times, it was difficult to handle the loneliness. So much life had been lived in that house in forty years it is impossible to describe it. Now, away from it, our lives would go on. In a strange way, we were fly-by-nights. I still can't drive by the house without feeling tremendously homesick.

8

What God Has Joined Together

∽

PROBABLY THE GREATEST SUFFERING THAT I CAME TO KNOW VICARIOUSLY was the pain of a man or woman whose marriage was breaking up. I began to do a great deal of marriage counseling, but I never could handle easily the pain that a woman felt when she became aware of her husband's infidelity, or of a man becoming aware of his wife's rejection. Sometimes, if the couple were willing to try, I'd ask, "Do you have any friends that are married?" Too often the answer would be, "Father, we don't know any couples who are happily married."

A young man I met at the prison asked me to visit him and his wife. When I stopped at their home after his release, I saw that they were very poor and were trying to make it in a one-room apartment with a shared bathroom. They'd been arguing when I came in; he wanted to continue the argument. They were going to break up and it was her fault. When they met and first started to live together, they had both liked country music. That made it easy to listen to the radio, and when they could afford to go out, they wanted to go to the same places. But now she'd changed. She didn't like country music any more. She had found some new friends while he was in jail, and now she only liked rock, which he couldn't stand. Where to begin?

A young man of twenty who was doing a ten-year sentence in a state penitentiary told me that he and his brother and sister had suffered tremendously as they were growing up. His father was an unpredictable alcoholic. His mother worked away from the home and was too worn out to be attentive to them at the end of the day. One day the mother left and took his sister with her. He was twelve years old, but he found his way across town to the apartment where she was living. Before he could explain anything, she told him that she didn't have room for him, that she didn't want him to come there. Her income was not enough for four and his sister needed her more than either of the boys did. He was stunned. Then he accused her,

"You don't love me."

She screamed at him, "Don't let me ever hear you say that again. How many television sets did we have?"

"Two."

"What were they like?"

"The big color set and the little black-and-white set."

"Which one did I take?"

"The little black-and-white one."

"Well, don't think that I didn't love you. I could have taken that big set instead, but I left it because I wanted you to be able to enjoy it."

Eight years later when he was telling me about it, he was still livid. The great sign of love that he was to hold on to so that he could never question her attitude was a color television set. She was utterly enraged that he didn't understand it.

He had a little over nine more years left in an overcrowded penitentiary that was becoming more overcrowded all the time through the zeal of law-and-order judges who wanted him to get the message, whatever that was.

∽

In one way or another addiction was part of the lives of most of the men I was seeing in prison. It was also at the heart of many of the broken families. Some, like the young man whose mother had left him the color TV, came from homes broken through alcoholism. Others were addicted themselves. Almost all of those addicted to alcohol shared one thing: the denial of the problem.

One man told me he was not an alcoholic, though he was in prison for drunken driving. I asked,

"Why don't you get out on bond?"

His wife wouldn't get him out. They were divorced.

"Did alcohol have anything to do with the divorce?"

"Well, yes."

His boss? He didn't have a job anymore. He'd lost it because of his drinking. His savings? He had none. His friends? None that really cared.

But he wasn't an alcoholic. As this conversation was repeated over and over with different prisoners, I found that they all had their own definition of alcoholism—one that didn't fit themselves. "I'm not an alcoholic. I don't need it all the time." "I'm not an alcoholic, I never drink in the morning." Or, "I never miss work on account of it." Or, "I only drink beer. Never touch the hard stuff."

The definition I use is simple: "An alcoholic is a person who cannot live a normal existence on account of alcohol." So what's normal? In the case of this prisoner, I said, "Look. Your wife is gone. Your job is gone. Your friends are gone. Your money is gone. Your reputation is probably gone. Your freedom is gone. If you had given up those things for the love of God you'd be one of the greatest saints that ever lived. And you think you can control alcohol?"

Then I went on to a line of thought that was cruel but valid. "Do you realize that everyone who loves you has been hurt?" I wouldn't let him look away or blame anyone else. I wouldn't even let him assume a self-pitying guilt that he would use to drop the subject or get rid of me. I just wanted to strip him of all the blaming of others that he used to defend himself, and leave the basic awareness, "I am a flop. A failure as a human being. Everyone who loves me gets hurt."

That is the powerlessness, the helplessness that of itself could be suicidal in a conscious living out of the unconscious suicide of a drinking career. A realization of powerlessness that could unmask the many forms of hypocrisy from the past. He couldn't hide in the mental escape that life would be fine if only he could jettison his whole past. And I was asking for a moment of honesty. "You're beat. You're hurting much. You've hurt many. You're powerless. You can't blame circumstances. You can't hope for a different set of circumstances to succeed. There's no opening on another planet. You're on this planet, and you need help."

When a person aching from the misery of his own life admits he's powerless with an interior acceptance, he's taken what AA calls the first step. Then he's honestly ready for the second step. He looks for help. A drowning person looks for a savior, not on his own terms. He's ready to surrender. "To surrender to God as I know him" in AA, is, for a Christian, to surrender to Christ.

But surrender can't just be a mental aspirin, "the power of positive thinking." If a child climbs to a porch roof and finds himself stranded, he may panic. If his father from the ground says, "Jump, I'll catch you," the child is afraid not only of the eight feet to the ground, but of the two-and-a-half feet to his father. The father repeats, "Jump." The moment the child jumps he is surrendering. He's found a frame of mind to relieve him of a lifetime of isolation on the roof. But his father still has to be there to catch him. Really. Safely. Lovingly.

It dawned on me gradually that *all* people have their own poison: alcohol, drugs, sex, money, prestige. To each his or her own. In some ways addictive substances are merciful in making clear the powerlessness of their victims quite quickly. Society is kinder in a cruel way to those whose lives are caught on more respectable reefs.

Over the years, I had the same conversation with hundreds of men and women. Almost always, it was one on one, partially to assault individual defenses and partially to protect the respectability of a person who fears not only to look at himself or herself honestly but also to let others see him or her. I needed to make clear to each one individually, "You are important." A failure perhaps, but an important failure, with an important future.

One man in prison whose alcohol was responsible for his failed marriage told me earnestly that he needed to convince his parole officer to let him get bond. His mind and his speech were moving constantly. He had old alcoholic problems: his wife had left him, taking their son with her, and returned to her mother's home. He had quit drinking, gotten a job, courted her again until she agreed to give their marriage one last try. They made a down payment on a trailer. Their marriage was going well. His job was going well. Life was beautiful.

Then he started to drink and got into new trouble with the law. Now he would lose everything if he didn't get out immediately. He would lose his job, and they would miss the next payment on the trailer. If they lost the trailer, his wife would have to go back to her mother, who would never let her come back to him again. Then his wife would be gone. His son would be gone. His job would be gone. His trailer would be gone.

After we spent some time together, I said,

"You know what you ought to do? Before you go to bed, kneel down and give God your trailer."

"What do you mean?"

"Well, what has you so upset is losing your trailer. God is all-powerful. Give it to him and tell him you'd like to have him keep it for you and your family, but if he wants it for someone else, that's all right too."

He was half puzzled, half angry.

"What do you mean, 'that's all right too?'"

"I mean if God didn't want you to have your trailer, you wouldn't want it, would you?"

"Why wouldn't God want me to have my trailer?"

I said, "That's not the point. The real point is, if God didn't want you to have that trailer, you wouldn't hold onto it, would you?"

He thought he would. He knew he would.

And I said, "There's your real problem. You can't trust God."

Then he went back to his cell. He talked to his cellmate for quite a while. He thought I was a nice guy but not quite with it. I had this basic problem that I didn't understand real life. He wrestled with the problem for two or three days. Then one Thursday evening he stopped fighting. He surrendered. He knelt down and gave God his trailer.

When he did, his whole attitude changed. He slept peacefully. He woke up happy. Friday was visiting day. His wife, whom he hadn't expected, came for a visit, and recognized the change immediately. The first thing she said was,

"What happened?"

He said, "You're not going to believe this, but last night I gave God our trailer."

As he was describing it to me, he said, "She looked at me like I was out of my mind, and said, 'Well, it was his all the time anyhow, wasn't it?'"

Again in describing the scene to me, he said, "I felt just like she slapped my face, because she understood all along what it took me so long to figure out."

That happened over thirty years ago. At least until ten years ago, when I saw him last, he was still sober . . . and peaceful.

∞

As I was working in prisons I ran into young men who in their teens had been involved in juvenile pornography. I wondered what effect such experiences would have on them, on their concept of the human race. Without exception, I found that their deeper disillusionment came from their younger childhood experiences. For the most part, they were defensive of those who had used them sexually, either homosexually or heterosexually. "At least they were kind. Somehow they cared." But in fact there were many who didn't survive when the adult that was seeking gratification expressed himself as the killer parent.

On the streets, many a strangely dressed man, many a bag lady, is making the statement, "I will not play your game." With the distance between them and their families, they wind up in prisons and mental institutions, in hospices, and under the stars—on the margins of a world that doesn't care for them, or at least doesn't know how to show care. They are an annoyance to our consciences. About them Christ will say, "You saw me sleeping near the subway, and walked right past."

Boys and girls, once needed for chores such as cooking and cleaning, for kindling and shoveling and dishes and canning, now find that their biggest contribution to the family—or its remnant—is to stay out of the way and amuse themselves. Then to be needed as a companion is a real joy. To be needed for sex seems a new experience, not so much for the sex, as for the being needed.

At the county prison one afternoon, a guard asked me if I would talk to one of the woman inmates. When I agreed, I asked what it was she wanted to discuss. He said, "I'm not sure she'll want to discuss it, but you'll see."

In the old prison the section for women was very small. Sometimes it would be empty for days, even weeks. It was on the second floor, and access was by a winding stairway. As she came down the stairs, I was surprised. Her hair was teased high. She had on dangling earrings and dark mascara. She had a midriff and tight toreador pants with sequins. Her shoes had platform soles. She posed her way down the stairs, as though she expected the guards and me to be livid with desire.

When we were alone, she relaxed. She was a call-girl, angry at the lawyer who had failed to get her out. I told her how out of place her makeup was. We went on to discuss dignity not only in prison but in life. She wasn't defiant in the least. After we talked, we prayed together. Her appearance and her attitude changed.

She got out on bond and for a while I didn't see her. Then one school day, when classes were changing, I was walking across Sixth Street. Around the corner came a convertible, bright shiny red. She was in the driver's seat. In appearance, she'd gone back to her old ways. There were two other girls in the car with her, similarly dressed.

She saw me and waved earnestly, yelling, "There's Father Peterson. Hello, Father Peterson." I waved and smiled. Students who were crossing the street looked at her and then back at me. I said, "Don't worry about it. She's my sister." And I laughed.

But she was my sister, as each man is my brother.

∞

The sense of the brokenness of so many of the men and women I was meeting only heightened my joy at being with people in love. All of my priesthood I have loved to assist at weddings. Sacramentally, a priest is to lead people in prayer into the presence of God. Sometimes in preparation there is much debris to be removed from the path. Either partner or both may have much forgiving to do in regard to significant people in their early childhood. They may have painful experiences of early dealings with church people or harsh images of the Church. They may need to come to grips with their own self-concepts—forms of deliberate ugliness they have tried to hide from themselves, or from others, or from God. To lead anyone through them takes great sensitivity and gentleness. To accept him or her afterward with a kiss of peace is to experience what it means to be a father. "You are my son. This day I have begotten you." "You are my beloved daughter. In you I am well pleased."

At a seminar I was teaching on marriage, a group of students was discussing the signs to look for to determine whether a given marriage would be happy. Toward the end of the discussion, George Titus, a student from India, said that he thought the whole discussion was foolish.

"In America, you look for signs like fireworks between two people. If you find them, then no matter what other reasons there are for regarding the marriage as foolish, you go ahead—and live with the mess. When I finish school, I'll go back to India and work on my career. When I think I'm ready to be married, I'll tell my parents. They'll pick out a girl. I will meet her and marry her three weeks later and have the happiest marriage of anyone in this room." Period.

The others were startled. Then one said, "That won't be a real marriage. You'll treat her like a pack animal. That's the way your parents will choose her." It was the only time I ever saw George angry. His parents loved him. They knew what he needed in a good wife, and that was way more than a pack animal. His mother and father had a deep respect for each other and a lifetime love. He calmed down and said, "The trouble with you here is that you look for some emotional excitement, call it love, and then tear it apart by trying to build a lifetime on it. In our country, we figure if we're going to live together for the rest of our lives, we might as well fall in love and enjoy our lives together."

His comments called to mind Dad's advice when I told him I was teaching a course on marriage: "You can't teach people anything about marriage. Just tell them that if they're ever going to be happy they have to give everything they have without counting the cost. Tell them if they ever wonder 'How much am I getting out of this?' they'll always think they're being cheated."

The awareness of the needs of others is central to a person's maturing. When someone says, "I want to be me" or "I want to be free," that person wants to ignore the needs of others without feeling guilty. That person means that he or she doesn't want to be mature. At the same time, the awareness of the freedom of those who have sacrificed to meet my needs brings with it eventually the awareness of being loved. We can't see love, taste love, or touch love. The only way we can realize that we are loved is by recognizing the signs of it in our lives. Where love is, God is.

Dad's outlook, and George Titus's view of marriage, sprang from having known the security and love of a home from childhood. But where to begin when a woman or a man has no experience of a stable marriage or even scorns the values on which it rests? During my teaching years, there were a number of students who had no faith, no religious background. Since it was a requirement that students take a course in religion, I taught a course on natural religion. One of the students in the course, Bill Benson, had a Jewish background but was an agnostic, hostile to religion. After a period of being resentful that he was required to take such a course, he started to listen. When we dealt with the question of the providence of God—which meant dealing with the problem of evil—he perked up and became interested, and we became friends.

A few years later I had a call from him. He'd met a marvelous girl. He called her Katie, and he wanted to marry her. She was a Catholic, and he had to agree about the children being raised in the Church, and she wanted to be married by a priest. Well, he still didn't like anybody telling him what to do about anything, but he'd agree if I could do the wedding. Their pastor agreed, and we had the wedding. It was just beautiful. He loved Katie so much he was tamed.

Some years later I was at a hospital one day, and Bill came running up to me near the elevator. He said, "Father, Katie's got cancer, would you come and pray with her?" It was the first time he ever asked me to pray. Katie had just beautiful faith; we prayed together, and she hadn't the least fear. Just where it came from I don't know. She was a beautiful gift.

She died. And some time after her death, Bill came up to me on the street and said, "Father I have to talk to you. I muffed it again." He told me that before Katie died he used to go and sit there in the hospital. But he was so down that one day she said, "Bill, it doesn't help either of us like this. I'll be all right, why don't you get some of your buddies and go out to the peninsula and just relax for awhile." So he did, he got two of his friends and they went. He no sooner got there when he knew something was wrong. He went racing back to the hospital and found the door closed. The nurses told him that Katie had died.

He went in by himself. He said he just wanted to lie down for a bit next to her body. A light came on, and he was annoyed that there was no privacy at all. But he looked up and the light wasn't on. He saw a marvelous golden cloud with green streaks through it. He told me, "I knew Katie was tellin' me something." He had said, "Katie I know you're tellin' me you're all right, but I don't want that, I want you!" He went on, "I yelled at her, when she was tryin' to be good to me." And he didn't know how he could undo that, but he wanted to know if I could understand that.

I asked him if he understood anything about the Communion of Saints.

"What's that?"

So I explained and said, "Have you ever read the New Testament?"

"No."

So I said, "Wait'll I go to the car." I returned and gave him a New Testament, and that made all the difference.

He came out to see me a few years later. He had cancer himself, but he wasn't afraid. I was worried how this would affect his thought of God's providence. He said, after the years he had with Katie he could never question God. And we prayed together.

A few months later I was at a mall, and he came running up with his two daughters. He took me away from them a little ways and said, "The doctor said I have only three months to live." I asked him about his faith. No problem. It was just so simple. And I asked him about the girls. He said that deciding that they would be Catholic was the best thing he ever did; they were going to be fine.

And he wasn't afraid about dying. So we just prayed a little bit to Jesus and then he joined the girls. And the last time I saw him he was looking back at me. Then he and the two girls were lost in the crowd.

∽

In the first years of my priesthood, when I was young and more efficient, I used to wonder why, if he loved suffering people so much, God wasted thirty years of the life of Jesus in the everyday repetitions of being a carpenter at Nazareth. As I came to know broken men and women and thought of Jesus with his own deep realization of his Father's love and the love of Mary and Joseph, the awareness grew of how much God needed Joseph and Mary for Jesus to achieve a stable humanity. It was not a moment or a few months of zapped-in splendor—Michelangelo's creation of Adam in the Sistine Chapel. It was years of simple growth, of being together through thousands of everyday crises.

One of the happiest memories of my life is an evening spent in Boston with a young couple whose wedding I was to have the next day. His name was Ed Freeman. He had come to Gannon on a football scholarship. His heart was at home with Maddie, his fiancée, a long-distance telephone operator. When the others wanted him to date or go partying, he wasn't interested at all. When they were to be married, I flew to New England.

After the rehearsal, we went to the apartment they were getting ready for themselves. It was only partially furnished and we sat on the floor as we talked. The presence of God in the room was overwhelming. They talked of their parents and grandparents with such joy and admiration. Their own priorities were built on what they had breathed in from their own families. It was such a privilege to ask the next morning, "Ed, will you take Maddie, here present, for your lawful wife?" And to hear that he would, and she would. Then to announce to one and all, "What God has joined together, let no man put asunder." That isn't poetry. What God has joined together, he can hold together.

9

*For This
Was I Born*

⬭

DURING THE EARLY YEARS OF MY PRIESTHOOD, I WAS SLOWLY
branching out farther and farther from teaching theology and English to
college students. I liked teaching and was a good teacher, counselor, and
friend to students. But the archbishop also assigned me to vocation work
and to teaching and preaching to the sisters of the diocese. The Erie
county prison was another ministry, as were Cursillo, Christian Family
Movement, Serra Club, and Catholic Daughters of America. One day
someone asked me, "What's your full-time job?" And I said rather plain-
tively, "I wish I could be full time at anything." Then I realized how self-
centered that was.

Occasionally, I had dealt with a man or woman who was emotionally
disturbed. If on a given day a disturbed man has an appointment with a
doctor and plans to get a haircut and possibly mail a letter, he is panicked
because there's too much to do. The faith to let God be God and to have
nothing to do but his will is a bridge to real peace and productivity. It
came to me that I could wake up the next day with only one thing to do—
and that was God's will.

Ten years into my priesthood, though, I began to question whether I
was looking for God's will or my own. I enjoyed everything I was doing
and I was doing it well. But was it all God's work—or mine? With many
people responding strongly and favorably to me in my different roles, it

was too easy to slip into the notion that it was all happening because of me. Many days my prayer would be shortened or almost left out. If a needy student came to my door, I always had time; but I wouldn't have time for a visit to the Blessed Sacrament.

I had heard about the Institute of the Sacred Heart of Jesus, a secular institute that required an hour of mental prayer daily, along with vows of poverty, chastity, and obedience. I was drawn to it especially for the promise of daily mental prayer. The more I knew of the institute, the more I wanted it. A requirement before final vows was to make a thirty-day retreat following the spiritual exercises of St. Ignatius Loyola.

I spent the thirty days at a huge estate near Franklin, Pennsylvania, which the White Fathers of Africa had recently acquired. Their novice master agreed to guide me. I found that I did not need time to unwind— the interior life was more absorbing that it had ever been. The community gave me a space for silence; the river and the hills and the trees helped bring me perspective; the chapel was alive. It was like beginning again.

Ignatius, who was culturally a noble and a Catholic, had come through a profound experience when he was wounded in battle and almost died. For the first time in his life he faced his mortality. Then as he began to recover, he wanted some light reading. All he could find were a life of Christ and some lives of the saints. As he read the life of Christ, he was appalled that he never really knew what Christ taught or what Christ wanted of him. His "vocation" as a soldier collapsed. He lost his sense of security and identity and had to face the question alone, "Who on earth are you?"

A "calling" is not a hidden set of marching orders. It is a process. Someone calls, someone hears. What happens afterward depends on the relationship between the two. St. Paul says that we have been taken prisoner by Christ, that he is the one who appoints pastors, teachers, healers, administrators—those who will carry on his work in his Spirit, by the power of his Spirit.

In retreat we need to ask "Who in heaven are you?" and "Who on earth am I?"

∽

My own vocation, my "calling" as a priest, I knew, was to lead people into the presence of God. As young priests returned to visit when I was in the seminary, we would look at them with admiration, welcome them joyfully, and share liturgy with them. We would sing the words of Psalm 110, "The Lord has sworn and he will not repent, 'You are a priest forever according to the order of Melchizedek.'" And often I thought what a beautiful tribute that was. God has made you a priest and he will never regret it.

Only what happens if the priest goes downhill; if he is effective in other things without leading people into God's presence; or if he is effective in nothing but survival? In the Old Testament Abijah laments the cheapening of the priesthood. "Anyone who comes with a bull and seven rams to get himself consecrated can become a priest of what is no god at all" (2 Chron. 13:9). Old Eli lived through the terrible sadness of seeing his sons, priests by heredity, using their role for self-centered purposes.

At first I had a static notion of "vocation," embodied in functions, with distinct ways of life. If someone accepted a vocation to be a priest or a banker or a farmer, his lifestyle was all laid out for him. He had simply to priest or to bank or to farm.

Moses, as a shepherd in Midian, could have called his care of sheep his vocation. He had a wife, two sons, a future to breathe in. At the burning bush he knew he was called to more, though he was by no means delighted at the idea. To return to Egypt because of the needs of his people was to risk everything that he valued. Until then, apparently he'd been able to shut out the voices of the runaway slaves. They were beyond the rim of his valley. He had other responsibilities that he knew he could handle. The entrapped descendants of Jacob were not aware of their own identity as a people, were not in any way united enough to help themselves or to cooperate in being helped. They were being tyrannized by a great political and military power in a land where Moses was wanted for murder.

And Moses reluctantly moved in a new direction with a faith that was real, but often without feeling the certainty of the everlasting arms.

Ignatius, after an extended retreat, invited others to share the journey of conversion in what became known as his spiritual exercises. As I began the journey, I found that it involved a tremendous stripping. The exercises cried out for a passionate indifference to the means by which one serves God and made clear that it is only in surrender that one can come to peace about whether he is following the will of God or his own whims.

As the journey continued, day by day, I was spending more and more time with Jesus, looking at his world and mine through his eyes. I began to be more in touch with his mental and emotional life—springing from his early life in a village. I knew that he was God; now I was realizing his responses more humanly. In Nazareth, without seeing how he would handle the authorities, he came to trust, "If this is the work God wants, he will supply what I need."

As I grew more in touch with Jesus' view of the world from Nazareth, I saw the religious vows of poverty, chastity, and obedience in a fresh way. For his hidden self to grow strong, Jesus too had to be stripped: to live as the poor and sick men and women he responded to, to mature emotionally beyond indulging any human whims, and to give up his own local identity and be obedient to his Father's voice leading to a future and a role that had no clear shape in the Jewish world around him. I saw that to surrender the feeding of one's own desires, to surrender control and a secure life by the standards of the flesh was not merely an option for religious men and women. It lay at the heart of Christ's way of living: "I do always the things that please Him." To that simplicity he called all Christians.

Jesus said that his sheep would hear his voice and would not follow the voice of a stranger. His voice was calling me to an unknown future. My "vocation" was not static, but was constantly unfolding in response to the voice of Christ in the poor and the broken. I no longer felt I had a roadmap.

But I wasn't afraid. Just grateful to be loved by God and called by him.

One of the exercises of Ignatius is a "contemplation for obtaining love." It involved a recalling of events in my life that had brought me to a realization of God's goodness. Each event was to be recalled, relived, savored, seen as a gift from God, and valued as a sign of his love.

I've never finished the exercise. Whenever I begin it, I find the renewed awareness of some marvelous moments of peace and joy. I have only to go back in memory to that first night at Paca Street, to the experience of being at home with the Blessed Sacrament when everything else was in darkness. I memorize moments that I'm fondest of.

Jesus has asked that at the center of all of my days, I remember his suffering and death—for me. "As often as you do this remember me." I proclaim his death. I have long since realized that I proclaim a thing only if it is important to me—and to those with whom I'm sharing it.

When I read the signs of God's love, I know his love so much that even when I'm not sure what he is doing, I know that Christ is doing it and therefore it is wonderful. He loves me too much to waste a minute of my life. But I realized that I needed more time for quiet prayer, for being-with-God who is always with me. Many "things" were not important, except people and God. But in that freedom I could see who I was. For this I was born. For this I came into the world.

It was exciting. And I was young again. And Christ was young again and exciting. The exercises meant living with Jesus and Peter and Andrew and James and John. They obviously had a great deal of courage in giving up their fishing business and their homes and the security of their way of life. But Jesus was very clear to them when he said, "Without me you can do nothing." They heard it but didn't know it. Even toward the end Peter said, "Why can't I follow you now? I will lay down my life for you." He was still depending on himself to do what he thought God wanted him to do—the take-charge fisherman on a new course of action, just like Paul, the take-charge Pharisee expecting to take a new course of action when he asked, "What do you want of me?"

Even with their decision to follow, however, they had to learn a new humility. They couldn't transfer the principles of life from the fishing business to the people-fishing business, and they learned very slowly the need for purity of intention.

Jesus taught them by living with them familiarly. He'd send them out for practice teaching. Then he'd get away with them into the open country. At Caesarea-Philippi they came to a concentration of faith that enabled Peter to acknowledge with the help of direct grace, "You are the Christ, the son of the living God." That didn't come from flesh and blood but from the grace inside him.

Besides leading them to faith, Jesus brought them to fuller self-understanding and required of them a new defining of priorities. "Whoever loves father or mother more than me is not worthy of me, and whoever loves son or daughter more than me is not worthy of me; and whoever does not take up his cross and follow after me is not worthy of me. Whoever finds his life will lose it, and whoever loses his life for my sake will find it."

As the days went on and the world diminished, it was easy and absorbing to spend time with the risen Christ—only a breath away from Peter in prison or Stephen being stoned or Paul in his journeyings. The promise of the living Jesus was that I would never be orphaned or deprived of his Spirit or condemned to a fruitless day. Poverty, chastity, obedience: a small price to pay for the immense freedom they bring. I saw my life through fresh eyes.

∞

At the time I made the thirty-day retreat, I was spiritual director at St. Mark's seminary, shaping young men for the priesthood. I realized that less than half of them would be ordained. Like Ignatius, they were culturally Catholic, without knowing within themselves who Jesus is or what he expects of them. I turned to shaping a spirituality of Christianity, rather than a spirituality of priesthood, one that reflected my growing sense that each one of us was called to a "vocation," that each one of us was called to lift our horizons to see the slaves beyond the rim of our valleys, that each one of us was called to share communion with Christ, to take time to rest and reflect and pray on the soil of our conversions. In silence. In loyalty to grace.

But I knew that carrying the gospel to people who had often heard it was certain to be interpreted by them in the same way their other teachers had lived it in their own lives. Children who learn the Beatitudes in homes that are yuppily indifferent to the needs of the poor are going to say "I know those things" and be annoyed that they are asked to learn again what they have never learned.

If it took near-death struggles and great pain to get Ignatius to listen to the words he was reading in boredom, it would take more than a brief sermon or some transient hearing in a three-credit course to awaken hearts to the power of the gospel. A thirty-day retreat can help a great deal to reveal the hidden brokenness that comes from depending too much on ourselves and not enough on God, from wanting to fix things, as though anything I was working on could be fixed. That revelation leads to an honest need for Jesus as Savior and then joy in the risen Christ, who is not only Lord but also friend.

I needed in every way possible to help people realize that Jesus is never Lord in a person's life unless he is chosen as Lord. God made Jesus Lord. Jesus never makes himself Lord by intimidation. He is so gentle; he calls and waits. The most Godlike thing anyone can do is make Jesus Lord in his or her own life.

I felt a strong call to go to the broken. They at least knew they couldn't row their own boats. The poor and the little could hear. The shrewd, the secure in their own world, needed first to realize their inadequacy before the gospel could get in. That might require the prophetic teaching of John the Baptist fighting the denial of the wise and the established; it might take some traumatic incident to make clear that the most important things in our lives are out of our control.

Afterward would come the teaching moment.

I knew that in teaching scripture I had to bring Christ into the classroom and then go beyond the classroom with retreats, student group living, service to the poor. I worried about seminarians and young religious who saw their "vocations" as institutional to be lived out in an upper-income lifestyle. As I searched for a means of bringing them to a way of prayer and a lifestyle that were deeply Christian, I kept returning to one image of Christ: living day by day with his small group of followers, with his friends—on the fringes of the structured world.

In those thirty days apart, in silence, I came to realize that I had to rethink the roles in which I had lived my priesthood. With the breaking of those conventional roles and a clear call to the poor and broken, the future was uncertain.

That too was exciting.

10

The Scars of Violence

ONE HOT SUMMER AFTERNOON, I HEARD A KNOCK AT MY OFFICE door and opened it to a very hostile black man, a road man in denim jeans, jacket, and hat. He was uncomfortable from the heat and apparently more uncomfortable from having to ask for help. The alias he was using was Floyd Shepard. Someone had told him he could get a meal from me. He demanded it in a challenging tone. I told him I'd be glad to help and started to write out a note. Just then it thundered, and his manner changed. He asked me if he could stay for awhile. I asked him in. As we talked, it began to rain. Each time it thundered, he quaked. Neither he nor I commented on his fear, but as it grew dark, he asked if I could help him find a place for the night. There was a vacant room right across from mine. I let him take it. We said a prayer together, and I wished him good night.

The next day he slept till after ten o'clock. In his relaxed mood he told me that he was a fugitive and that this was the first time he had slept peacefully in over a year. Then, hesitantly, he asked whether he could stay for just one more night. He told me he was a veteran. He had gotten into difficulty with the law in California. He didn't think he was guilty, but in that part of California there was much hostility between Latins and blacks. The Latins had the upper hand, so he knew he wouldn't get a break or even get justice.

I knew he had come a long distance from the angry begging of the night before to the trust he was showing in dropping his cover. I didn't want to push him too far. But I asked him if he would let me call the District Attorney in the county where he was wanted. I'd try to see whether anything could be worked out, so he wouldn't have to spend the rest of his life as a fugitive. His anger sprang back in force. He knew this had been too good to be true. All the time, I was setting him up.

When he calmed down, I assured him that what we discussed was between us and that I would never discuss any of it with anyone except by his permission. For some time that seemed good to him. Not long after, he brought up the subject. He was lonely. He couldn't spend time with the people who had been important to him because the police would find him. Every time a knock came on the door of any room he was in, he froze. But he knew if I called, they would come after him. I told him I couldn't promise that nothing would go wrong, but that his future was completely dismal in his present circumstances, and I would like to try. Finally, he agreed.

I called the District Attorney's office in Los Angeles, talked to an assistant D.A., had his assurance that what we discussed would be in confidence, and that he would take no action without talking to me again. He knew nothing of the particular case, and would have to investigate before he could discuss options.

The next day, two F.B.I. agents came to my office with a warrant for Shepard. They knew I was in touch with him, and they wanted me to take them to him. I refused. They became threatening. I was harboring a criminal. That in itself was criminal. They could have me arrested. Without any defiance, I told them to go ahead and arrest me. I was appalled that the assistant D.A. had broken his word. I was not about to break mine. Then they became paternal and protective. This guy was dangerous. He wouldn't hesitate to slit my throat. I told them I didn't regard him as dangerous, and although I would not take them to him, I would try to bring him to them. I got another lecture on his shrewdness and my stupidity, although that wasn't the word they used, and they left—without arresting me.

When I told Floyd, he said he was going to run. I pleaded with him, promised to get a lawyer and even to fight extradition, but he was too afraid. He couldn't trust anyone in the legal system. He left. So did part of my heart. Five or six hours later, he called. He couldn't go on running. He agreed to turn himself in if I would go with him.

I investigated the procedure, then the two of us went to the F.B.I. office. One of the agents who'd visited me was there. His amazement was transparent—but by then I shared enough of Floyd's fear that I couldn't enjoy the triumph. We went together to the county jail. Floyd was hardly able to speak. Through the bars he was a crushed child—his eyes made clear that he was half afraid that I'd abandon him and forget him.

The federal marshal had told me ahead of time that if Floyd turned himself in, he could probably let him out on a $1,000 cash bond while he was fighting extradition. That was $950 more than I had, but I was able to borrow it. Floyd was out in two days. He had a good mind, was eligible for the G.I. Bill, and by September he was taking a few courses at Gannon.

He trusted neither his own family, nor Chicanos, nor whites, nor God. The anger he had expressed when he first asked for food, he expressed to many others. I knew he didn't belong in our dormitories.

A few weeks before I met Floyd, Gus Hicks had come to my office with a politeness and sense of humor that never failed him and a neediness that embarrassed him tremendously. He too was a veteran. He too was black. He had a bad problem with alcohol and a physical problem—a kind of weakness and twitching of his legs that made it impossible for him to stand for long or to do heavy work. We talked for a while. As he relaxed, it was easy to see he had a deep faith and a loving family behind him. Only he felt that he had disappointed them seriously. I asked whether he'd mind if I prayed for him. I put my hands on his head and prayed, simply and thoughtfully. The next day he was back. His legs had stopped quivering. He was at peace.

Gus was admitted to Gannon, and he and Floyd became roommates in my living room. Whenever he was there, there was laughter. He and Floyd were good for each other: Gus was the elder brother who could tame Floyd's moods. Before he left, Gus told of a minister in his hometown who deceived people—he put a platform under water to make it appear he could walk on water. He'd get girls so emotionally involved at a Sunday afternoon prayer meeting that any guy could go to bed with them. His mother was beyond all this. She was loving, sincere, faithful; the minister had turned him off, and he'd let his faith slide.

Gus and Floyd became the center of a circle who'd drop by and have animated talks. One day Floyd was denying intensely that he had any Christian faith. He said, "Jesus never did anything for me." Then he interrupted himself, fairly quietly, "Well, almost never," and went on, "So, why should I do anything for him?"

When the others were gone, I asked him, "Floyd, why did you say 'Almost never?'"

He said, "I figured you'd pick that up, but I don't want to talk about it."

"But, Floyd, I do."

We were alone, so he told me he'd been using hard drugs in Vietnam, and really didn't care about anything. Once he and nineteen others had been ambushed and were under heavy fire. He promised Jesus that if he got out alive, he'd never take hard drugs again. Just two of them survived. At first, he was afraid he'd promised too much. Then the other guy said,

"Did you see what happened? The shells were coming in a direct line toward the ditch you were in. When they were almost there, they went around in a half circle. Then they picked up in a straight line again."

"After he said that," Floyd told me, "I knew the Lord had spared me and was telling me that he spared me. I kept my word. I never monkeyed around with drugs again."

From there we went on to what he was spared for.

Twice I went with Floyd to extradition hearings at the county courthouse. There were many procedural delays. Sometimes Floyd would forget all about the danger they threatened. His lawyer was most interested in the case and in him, but so were the people from California.

Twice I was in court with him—he seemed almost in shock. He'd put his hands on his stomach and rock back and forth. On the stand, he seemed drained of vitality. He answered very softly. When we got outside, he asked, "What happened?" I thought at first he was confused about the legal terms, but it wasn't that. He knew the law much better than I did. It was as if he had been in a blackout.

The procedures dragged on so long that he was able to finish Gannon while we were still fighting extradition. Legally, that's impossible, but his attorney told me there was nothing further he could do. The next step was for Floyd to go out to California, and present himself at the alderman's office where the case had started. All I had to do was convince Floyd.

That wasn't easy. But it happened. He made the trip on his own. The matter was handled in less than an hour's time at the office of the District Justice, who was equally impressed at what Floyd had done, the freedom of his return, and the shabbiness of the case against him.

Floyd married and went on with his life. About every five years, he calls me.

∞

As the nation was rocked by interracial violence in the late sixties, the images of anger and destruction touched most homes in America. One December morning in 1971, Gannon woke up seething with incendiary tensions. A white student had been found unconscious, mugged, in one of the dorms. Tines of an Afro comb had been found—one in his neck, another penetrating the soft pouch surrounding his eye. It was not at first clear that he would live. In the panic surrounding his discovery, it seemed likely that if he did live, he'd be partially blind, or partially paralyzed. As part of an all-out war that seemed imminent, a few of the white students had equipped themselves with ropes for lynching.

Father Nash, the president, dismissed classes early and sent the students home for the Christmas break. Everyone needed breathing time.

Then began a marathon of meetings. As I went to one after another, my resentment deepened. We were accomplishing nothing. We were pooling our ignorance and having someone take notes of the stupidity. As the minutes piled up, the time of the semester break was ticking away. A time bomb that no one knew how to defuse.

I proposed that we set up a live-in for black students and white students to discuss our problems and try to find solutions.

It was arranged as a one-week course during the break, with fifteen black students, fifteen white students, and six live-in faculty. Dr. Lundy, who had conducted pressure sessions in interracial struggles for police departments, agreed to supervise the confronting sessions. There was much apprehension. All the rage and tension would be concentrated in this one island.

Fifteen white students registered, thirteen black students registered, and then, one by one, the faculty members withdrew. Dr. Lundy would commute from home. I was the only one who would live in. Finally, twenty-eight of us moved into a building together—fifteen whites, twelve blacks, and me—to spend a week together.

It was the cruelest week of my life.

We arrived on Tuesday evening. The students split into two groups, racially divided, to plan strategy. The opening session was set for nine o'clock the following morning. About 7:30 in the morning I had a call from Dr. Lundy. He had the flu and wouldn't be able to come.

The black students came smoldering with the violence of 250 years of repression by whites. They opened with anger, just this side of rage. The whites agreed that there had been immense injustice, but none of them felt responsible for it, nor did they feel bound to answer for it. The frustration was nearly complete. Then, as a group, they turned their anger on the college, where on one level or another, they all felt oppressed.

I found myself in the role of the institutional spokesman. It brought home to me how much I had been simply a spectator to the movement of the school. I had gone on teaching. I had counseled students. I was busy, my work fruitful. But many of the blacks who now came were from big cities, especially Philadelphia. I gave no thought to the jolting effect on them of such a changed lifestyle. Most of the whites who lived on campus were from the small towns of northwestern Pennsylvania. The students came from two different worlds.

Some of the blacks resented Christianity. It had sat passively by and watched the slave trade; their parents, their grandparents were Baptists or fundamentalists, passive and accepting in the face of injustice. Theology, philosophy, history, literature—all were taught as a white straitjacket they did not want to put on. We staggered through several sessions of raw hostility.

In one session the students did some role playing. Strangely, the anger of the blacks was shifting from a generic racial anger to harshness against

Gannon and their present situation. In one skit, a young black student played Father Pete. He was wearing a cassock, a large crucifix around his neck, and a constant smile.

Students came to him separately with some critical problems. Always he was kindly, told them to trust God, and blessed them on their way—apparently unaware of the depth of their discouragement and safe from any concern that would require him to intervene or put his unruffled calmness at stake.

The one who was mimicking me occasionally would glance over to see how I was taking it. He was not sarcastic a bit. Later we became very close. But the message was clear. Neither Father Pete nor the gospel that came from his lips had anything to say that would seriously deal with the problems of the black students.

Each day I said Mass in the chapel, but no one else came. I could not say one word about Jesus. I wasn't ashamed or afraid to; I just knew they wouldn't hear me. Whatever I said would fit into the mold of the professional academic. It would be fake.

This was what bothered me most. I had offered my life to Christ's service—about that I knew I was sincere—and these people were entrusted to me as part of that service, yet I could not mention Christ. I felt trapped. I had betrayed, or been betrayed. I had painted myself into a corner.

One day a few of the black students came to me to see whether they could go to a basketball game Gannon was playing in Buffalo. It was the first time they'd spoken to me without intense hostility. They needed to get away from the situation for awhile, but I knew the whites would want to go too. I thought the trip and the game might relax them and unify the group. So I said I'd try.

When I called the offices at Gannon, I was appalled. No money in the budget for it. Even if there were, I'd have to apply in triplicate. What about insurance in case anything happened. The triplicate application would have to go through several offices, and some administrators were away. I damned the torpedoes, ordered a bus, and let them go. And the trip did relieve tension.

By the next day they were showing more respect to each other, and to me, but anger at the institution seemed deeper and was expressed with a clearer focus. I invited the president to come and hear their views. At Father Nash's arrival the students reverted to rage: to them, he embodied all the oppression and insensitivity of the institution. The week was nearly over, and I was dejected.

Saturday afternoon, a few of the white students came to Mass. It was the first time since we had come that we prayed together. Afterward, some of the black students held a seance in their own part of the building.

The two caucuses wanted to end with a game. I don't recall the name, it might have been "birdshit." It involved guessing, and taking a drink of beer for guessing wrong. It seemed harmless enough. I was bored, discouraged, exhausted. About midnight, I excused myself and went to bed. The next day was our final day. We had to wrap up the sessions, clean up, and drive back to Gannon. The small consolation I had was that in the midst of so much hostility, none of the students had left, none of them was maimed.

When I woke up in the morning and went downstairs, I found the students still playing. But the mood was changed. There was no black or white, male or female. The air was clear. They had accepted one another. They even smiled at me. They'd been up all night and needed rest. We set the time for the final sessions in the early afternoon. They went to bed.

I went to chapel. There I had one of the most profound experiences of my life. First, I saw clearly the institutional failure in the relationship with the students. The college was small enough to be human and personal. It had been so with Floyd, with Gus Hicks. But before my eyes, it had grown impersonally institutional, and I had sat by. Advisors were quoting rules defining the possible, the impossible, reverently protecting the structure while sometimes crushing the individual. In my individual friendships I tried to encourage each one to do his best and to keep confidence in God. It was easy. It was also inadequate.

There in the chapel I saw too that decades and centuries of oppression and rejection of blacks had spawned that hostility and left such deep emotional scars. Scars in terms of self-concept, of identity, of the ability to trust. To speak of honest community meant dealing honestly with all those scars.

Then came an insight on a deep level of the relationship of grace and free will. The insight was blinding. Christ wanted from each of us love freely given. Love that required self-discipline and leads to the inner life that would enable anyone to give up possessing things, holding fast to identities, and life itself. That was Christ's love, brought to each of his people. Parents, structures that did not want to fail—or be regarded as failing—could enforce conformity. If they wanted acceptance, and ease, they could indulge the self-seeking of each one entrusted to their care. They could live and put to death. They could live and let die. But no family, no institution that loses confidence in the grace of God can help its members come to the full humanity that belongs to any man or woman who loves freely and unselfishly.

After a while, the fireworks stopped. I was just there. Alone without being alone. Touching everything without doing everything. I didn't want to move.

But I knew someone had brought my mail from Gannon. Several weeks before the live-in started, I had noticed at the prison that a group of Jesus people were doing some remarkable work. They touched some men that I couldn't reach at all. I dismissed it as emotional and transitory, but when so many people warned against the live-in and I had the strong sense that Christ wanted it to go ahead, I made up my mind that if somehow—against all human expectations—the group came together and someone gave testimony to the Spirit, I would investigate a charismatic course of Life-in-the-Spirit.

When I opened the top letter of my mail, it was an invitation to a Life-in-the-Spirit series that was beginning that evening at the Mercy Mother House. I knew I would be exhausted, but I just said, "Yes, Lord." By then the students had begun to stir.

At the final session, I wanted to explain the awakening that I'd experienced. I opened myself in a way that left me vulnerable—and realized that most of them didn't really care. That hurt me deeply but also confirmed in me that what was needed was not words but action. We broke up the session; the students cleaned and packed and still there was neither black nor white.

The second night back in school I got a phone call—there'd been a fight between a black student and a white student. I groaned inwardly;

it seemed the worst was upon us. But I was no longer bewildered or afraid. This was a specific problem. If we acted quickly, directly, we could handle it.

It came to me almost immediately that there were five people in the administration who would have to take action. But an ordinary meeting of all five would take three days notice to accomplish. I was afraid that would be too late, but as I left the dorm to go to the administration building, I ran into all five—one after another—and told them what they would have to do. Each one agreed.

I knew what was happening was beyond coincidence, but I also knew that God in his providence does not relieve us of the responsibility of acting. Abraham was not a puppet in the hands of God. They were friends. Each one gave everything.

On the way back from class, I saw a group of about twenty black students assembled in a lounge, obviously planning their strategy. Of the twenty students gathered, only two had been at the live-in. But as I came into the meeting, they made way for me. I told them the facts, told them what the school administrators had agreed to do, and how they could help the school and themselves. They listened. We all knew by now the difference between honesty and pacification.

Prior to the live-in, I would have considered walking into a meeting of black students as an invasion of their privacy. And prior to that week, I'd have waited to see what the administration would do in the face of a problem that belonged to the institution.

Tired as I was from the live-in, I went to the opening seminar of the Life-in-the-Spirit series—on the same Sunday that the live-in ended. The speaker was simple, open. He and the others in the weeks that followed were showing how the basic gospel was addressed to each human being. When Peter preached that great sermon on Pentecost, he made clear that we are in the messianic era, that the Messiah the Jews expected was Jesus of Nazareth, whose credentials from his heavenly Father were proved by many miracles, and whose death was not a negation of God's plan but its fulfillment. Then Jesus became Lord and wanted to bless people with his Spirit.

When the people who accepted those truths asked, "What should we do?" he told them they needed a change of heart—a depth conversion. They needed to be baptized for the forgiveness of their sins, and they would receive the Holy Spirit.

On the fifth evening of the series the team that was presenting the material—and others—prayed for each of the candidates. When they prayed for me, the experiences at the end of the live-in were renewed, but likewise I had a tremendous desire to be alone. It was the kind of yearning I had had at the monastery of Our Lady of the Holy Spirit, when I decided to ask to be released from diocesan priesthood to the Trappists.

After a while, the group was rejoicing, some speaking in tongues, some crying, some laughing, all of us singing. The others eventually went out for coffee.

I wanted to be alone, so I stayed in chapel. A bit later, a woman came in and sat down next to me. She said the Lord was giving me a gift of healing—especially for people who were deeply disturbed emotionally. Often, she said, it would be connected with the sacrament of Reconciliation.

I had been baptized in the Spirit years ago—kneeling by the statue of Our Lady on the grounds of Paca Street, removed only by a brick wall from the red-light district. At the time, I had assumed it was an experience that happened to all seminarians. Sadly, it is not.

I knew that neither conversion nor baptism-in-the-Spirit is a one-time terminal "zapping." Conversion is a lifetime process. There are plateaus in the gift of the Spirit—both in prayer, and in ministry. They continue to happen and continually demand loyalty. The inner clamor of being too important or too busy can choke up the process. So can the outer clamor—so can the ugliness of the desert or the tumult of the city.

∞

The violence we faced at Gannon was only a small echo of what spilled into the news each evening as the sixties drew to a close. On the streets, in the prisons. The letters I received from prisoners spoke of it more and more.

"I'm sorry to say that depression, violence, wasted time, and suicide, both carried out and attempted, is very much growing here." The day before this letter was written, one inmate had been beaten by another with a pipe. Another had been raped. He continues: "This is a war zone. It is no place for the weak. . . . They brought a 16-year-old kid in this week, he's got life. That's a crime."

I don't think I could survive in prison—without saying Mass and with no place to hide from sound. One of my friends told me he'd spent years in prison in his younger days, then some years on the street, and then returned to prison. The change surprised him. Now there was constant noise, twenty-four-hour sound: radios, television, arguments, rapping, rapping, rapping—noise. Never any letup.

At the end of the period of student rioting and protesting at Berkeley, I spent a summer there. After one session, we had to find shelter from the tear gas that erupted from the cans the police were shooting in our direction. Needing some rest and quiet, at the end of the sessions, I borrowed some camping gear and drove to Yellowstone National Park. Anyplace I could camp, there were wall-to-wall people. I left. I found no beaches in California where I could camp, so I drove south to the Baja. I had the radio on as I was entering Mexico. Neil Armstrong was just taking a very important step for mankind. The eagle had landed.

Tijuana was cluttered and harsh and noisy. Without stopping I drove to Ensenada and kept driving a hundred miles beyond, until the highway became a cow path. There I found a beach where I lived for three days without seeing another human being. I thought it would take me several days to unwind. I found I could become a beachcomber in no time.

I cannot remember ever being so jealous of my consciousness. The nights were so beautiful, I didn't want to go to sleep. The waves kept rolling in, sometimes with the moonlight playing on them, sometimes just as ghostly sounds. I woke for the sunrise, the coming to life of the earth in every bit of grass, every rock, every sand dune. Almost always, there was a row of birds flying along the horizon, an unending procession. I couldn't tell what kind they were, couldn't tell where they had been or where they were going. Of course, they didn't know those things about me either. In my sadder moments I wondered how soon Ensenada would become like Tijuana. The new highway was creeping along, bringing with it civilization, golden arches, and great signs that say, "Don't park here unless you're getting a divorce."

I'm not about to get a divorce just to get a parking place. It was only in my sadder moments that I verged on the cynical. In my better moments, I was at peace. I knew the Lord wanted me to rest and, as always, was pampering me with the lavishness of his love. Never for a minute did I envy Neil Armstrong on the moon.

But I prayed for my friends in prison who couldn't find ten minutes of solitude, and wished earnestly that any one of them could have had the three days.

11

Be Still, and Know
That I Am God

∞

IN 1972 I CELEBRATED THE TWENTY-FIFTH ANNIVERSARY OF MY
ordination to the priesthood. The last time Marie and I had been away
together was a quick trip to New York City when I was in the seminary. I
wanted to do something for her and thought it was a good idea to take a
trip every twenty-five years. She told me that the only place she really
wanted to go was the Holy Land. So we found ourselves transported to
Palestine.

In Israel, each day had its individual glory. I honestly did not antici-
pate it, but each shrine carried its own grace. For years I had known that
people mattered and prayer mattered. Houses, celebrations, fireworks,
cars, meals, things left me cold. Sharing the mind of another human
being could rivet my full attention and touch me indelibly with surprise.
Prayer could be overwhelming.

But Israel held the places and images of the scripture stories I'd been
nourished on from childhood—images that shaped my sense of the holy.
And my sense of the priesthood.

As we wound our way through Palestine, so much of it stark in its dry-
ness, the desert, the rugged terrain suggested that life is an unfriendly
labyrinth. One evening we stayed at a motel on the edge of the Negeb,
the great desert. Except for the building, there was only sand. As the sun
was going down, gusts of wind started to circulate. In the moonlight,
shadows seemed to waver in various shades on the sand. The desert held

out not the least invitation to enter. The proper legend would have been, "Leave all hope behind you who enter here." It must have taken a powerful weight of oppression to have unsettled the runaway slaves of Egypt enough to follow Moses into the desert. The hostile, unknown territory required a detailed roadmap to avoid being permanently lost. The roadmap to be memorized was the Law that regulated each day. It gave certainty at the price of freedom.

We went to Bethlehem. While the huge tomb of Rachel spoke of loyalty to the past, soldiers with machine guns on a number of rooftops brought us into the present; but the site itself brought us to the eternal.

The traditional site of the stable isn't much: dark, cavelike, a number of candles, a silver star on the floor. Not much. But then, except for the Incarnation, there isn't really much on the planet that is much. What mattered was an acceptance of the grace of the Incarnation, not especially emotional, not requiring words.

There was one Word. That was God's word. "And the Word was God." Some of the many people crowding through left after a while. Every so often another tour group would erupt through. Marie and I just stayed, without saying anything, because there was nothing to say. The longer I live, the more I like people who don't say anything when there's nothing to say.

In Nazareth we found that much of the village was so plain, there was nothing to erase to be back in the first century. At a fairly new church, I offered Mass. But Mary's *fiat* was what I was looking for: the message, the being there where God wants me to be—instead of a one-sided covenant where we are in charge and our ideas are incarnated. We want God to say *fiat* to our plan.

In this village Jesus was raised with the Mosaic Law, the great roadmap through a harsh terrain. Not with some miraculous foreknowledge of everything that would take place in his life, which would be a kind of cheating, but here, where Mary washed their clothes with the other women of the village and carried water home from the well, "he grew in age, and wisdom, and grace." And he *learned*. When he said his first words, they were in Aramaic. And when he was fascinated by boiling water and reached toward it, and Mary said "Don't," he didn't know why.

Here, at the crossing of several caravan routes, many Gentiles would pass through. If he wanted to talk to them, Mary would have grabbed him away. A good Jew didn't associate with Gentiles. It was the Law, the road-map. Don't associate with the Gentiles—don't mix with the Canaanites in the new Promised Land. These lessons, taught to all Jewish children, were imprinted on his mind.

Years later, during his ministry, when a Canaanite woman approached him and said, "Son of David, have pity on me. My son is troubled by a demon," he gave her, at first, no word of response. When she persisted, he said that his mission was to the lost sheep of the House of Israel, in honest obedience to the Law he was taught at home.

But she begged him, "Help me Lord."

And he said, "It is not right to take the food of sons and daughters, and throw it to the dogs."

"Please, Lord, even the dogs eat the leavings that fall from the master's table."

And Jesus was amazed at her faith. Jesus opened to a new insight that carried him to a level that would be hard on his mother. He showed growth. In being touched by her faith, Jesus learned to step beyond the roadmap, to respond to the spirit of God in people he was taught to shun.

This insight brought to mind an incident that occurred when I was driving home to Erie late one afternoon, and I saw a man in his fifties or sixties hitchhiking. You could see the perspiration under his arms, and I stopped to pick him up. As soon as he got in the car I thought, "I made a mistake. He smells."

He had hitchhiked up to Erie from someplace a couple hundred miles away because he'd heard there was work available in the area. He had spent two days looking for work but hadn't found any. I began to think, when you're hitchhiking, looking for work, you're not able to stay at a motel with a nice shower. You're not able to take three changes of clothes when you're on the road. The more I listened to him, the more I thought what an admirable man he was. But I had almost been kept from seeing the splendor that was there, by his smell.

One of our stops in the Holy Land was the port of Joppa. Many of the buildings and streets had been restored. There on the Mediterranean was the home of Simon the Tanner, where Peter had had the vision of the clean and unclean animals. He was on the rooftop praying at midday. He saw a sheet let down from heaven containing all kinds of animals. A voice reached him, "Take and eat." In perfect obedience to the parent wisdom that had molded his own childhood, the same that had molded Jesus, he refused. "Nothing unclean has ever passed my lips." And the voice returned, "What God has called clean, let no man call unclean."

He was stung. He puzzled. The Law was from God, so he could not break the Law. Yet it was God who was speaking. With the coming of Cornelius's messengers, Peter knew he was to break out of the Law. At Joppa, looking out on the great sea surging without restraint, Peter, who probably visited it only a few times in his life, was being told to take off his straitjacket, to reach out and respond to the mind of God. Reality didn't have to be dissected and labeled. Each one in the church entrusted to him was real, personal, individual. Every one had wounds and scars that needed to be bathed and healed.

Jesus asked nothing he would not do himself. "Come, *follow me*," into God's presence.

When we left the Holy Land, we went to Athens. On our first night we ate on the roof of a hotel to the accompaniment of pleasant voices and light and honest plunking of string music. The moon rose over the Parthenon with a stateliness that made the twentieth century seem vulgar. All around us were order and proportion and beauty steeped in agelessness. On a cruise through the Aegean, the water was deep blue verging on purple; each island where we stopped had a distinct culture, a distinct history. Sometimes the great cliffs that surrounded them were chalk white, sometimes just grey rocks as on the Maine coast. Each seemed itself, confident of the priority of the moment in which it lived.

The whole was so tremendously transient. All the meaning that individual events could pile up was no more than a tombstone waiting for an epitaph that the wind and the rain would quickly erase—except insofar as it was an anteroom to eternity.

∞

Over the years in my working with more and more broken people, with the number of people I was seeing and the multiplicity of jobs I held, when I was aware of being irritated at a man or woman I was dealing with, I knew it was not their fault but mine. I needed to rest. I needed time for prayer. I knew that to recognize God's presence in the moments of our lives, we have to take time to think about it.

In the Second Book of Kings, Naaman, a Syrian general suffering from leprosy, came to Israel bearing gifts to pave the way for a healing he'd heard he might find. Elijah the prophet didn't even come out of his hut, but sent word that the general should go and bathe seven times in the water of the Jordan. Naaman was insulted and started to leave, but his servants convinced him to give it a try. He was cured.

When he returned to the hut with his gifts, Elijah refused to accept them. Naaman then asked if he might take two loads of dirt with him so that in the future, he could worship on the ground where he had had his healing, on the ground of his conversion.

God had touched my life profoundly, gently, repeatedly, had brought me to moments of conversion, moments of holiness. I needed to take time and rest in them. It is not only at the burning bush that one needs to be humbled and attentive.

Many a time in the years since Paca Street, I have been aware of Jesus walking with me, sharing my life, praying with me, using my hands and my mind. In the splendor of Rome and Greece, I had new glimpses of the glories of humanity leading to the glory of God. Especially at Mass each day, the whole world of the moment focused on the eternal, and I knew that I could not come to the Father, except through Jesus. But with him it was possible to taste heaven, which is simply to give the praise of the heart to the Father and to the Spirit and to Christ the Spouse.

Only in Israel I had a deeper awareness of walking with Jesus, of listening to him in the Sermon on the Mount, of going inside his mind at Gethsemane, or of spending the night in the open on a hill in Galilee. Whoever said the geography of Palestine is the fifth gospel spoke well.

Sadly, for many tourists, that grace is easily eroded.

☙

A lasting image of my time in the Holy Land was our visit to the heart of old Jerusalem, to the ruins of the Temple, where Jewish people pray reverently at the Wailing Wall—the remains of Solomon's Temple, the reminder of the covenant. The guide took us to two hills and talked with rising enthusiasm of the significance of those walls during the Six-Day War. As he spoke, I looked to the side. There was the Garden of Gethsemane. And Jesus wept.

It was not a plea for civil rights that brought Jesus to crucifixion, but cleansing of the Temple. Priests, still repeating the old ways in the huge new structure of Herod the Great, were offering sacrifices. Jesus knew he could have broken with the society of his time by assaulting racial injustice or the care of the sick or the treatment of women. But he chose to use the cleansing of the Temple as the event that made a permanent break from the established Jewish leaders. Once he had done it, it moved like a steamroller to his death.

He left the Temple over which he had wept. It was a lonely farewell.

Then he turned to the strange band of followers that had formed around him. He knew their fears, the threat of his own coming death. His last night he wanted the common bond of their being together before God, singing the traditional psalms, recalling the covenant: "I have desired to eat this pasch with you before I suffer."

In prison, a criminal about to be executed can choose a last meal. He has a little bit of freedom. He can pick out the dinner music. But the meal is often steak or lobster—a sad statement, when it is anything short of a gathering of friends sharing love and mutual encouragement on their journey. In the midst of his own conflict, Jesus, a carpenter—not a priest by heredity—led those willing to be with him into the presence of God.

> . . . the time will come—indeed it has come already—when you are going
> to be scattered, each going his own way
> and leaving me alone.
> And yet I am not alone, because the Father is with me.
> I have told you all this
> so that you may find peace in me.
>
> (John 16:31–33 [*New Jerusalem Bible*])

In this last sharing of a meal, he leads them into God's presence by bringing them close to him, to comfort them. But his Father is so present to him that he seems almost to forget that they are there. In this way, Jesus showed them what it means to live in his Father's presence:

Father, the hour has come.
Glorify your Son,
so that your Son may glorify you:
so that, just as you have given him power over all humanity,
he may give eternal life to those you have entrusted to him.
And eternal life is this:
to know you,
the only true God,
and Jesus Christ whom you have sent. . . .
They were yours and you gave them to me. . . .
It is for them that I pray.
I am not praying for the world
but for those you have given me,
because they belong to you.
All I have is yours
and all you have is mine,
and in them I am glorified.
I am no longer in the world,
but they are in the world,
and I am coming to you.
Holy Father, keep those you have given me true to your name,
so that they may be one like us. . . .
Consecrate them in the truth. . . .

> (John 17:1–17 [*New Jerusalem Bible*])

At the time of my own greatest yearning, when I was most shaken loose, there were these words of Christ, the Lamb of God, the baptizer in the Spirit, the priest who could lead from any and all confusion into the presence of God.

Part Three

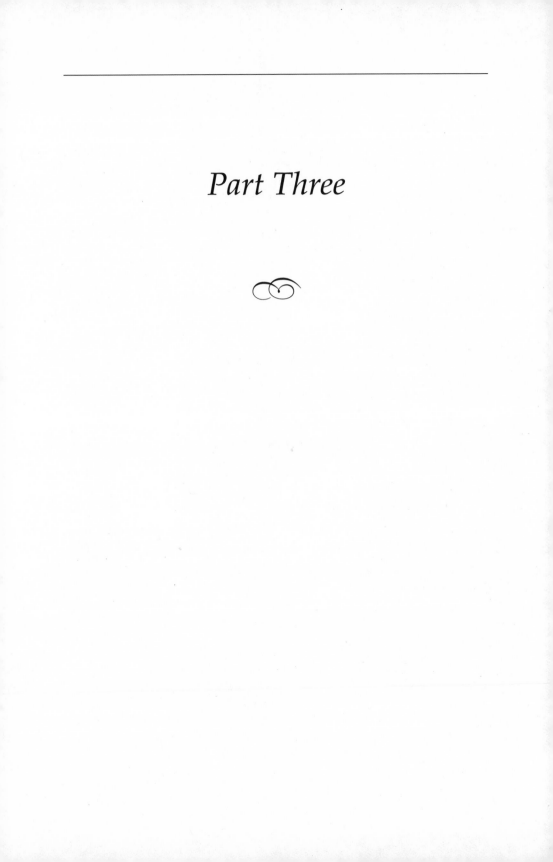

12

Blackie Sullivan and the Garbage Cat

ONE SUMMER I DECIDED TO RENT A HOUSE FOR MEN WHO WERE recently released from jail and had no place to go. After guaranteeing that I'd be responsible for damages, I moved in. Within two weeks seven ex-prisoners were living there, one or two in their twenties, but mainly men between forty-five and sixty-five. It was a student house during the year, belonging to the Thomas More Club and used by the men in our spiritual formation program—the ones who had visited the Trappist monastery. The day after the residents move, a fraternity house is ordinarily a disaster. The men cleared it, and kept it clean. The neighbors may have wondered, but no one complained.

For the men, it was very different from living in one room in a cheap hotel with a smuggled-in hot plate and a neighboring bar the closest invitation to companionship. A couple of the men could cook and enjoyed it. I suppose the hardest work I had that summer was helping the men learn to eat together. They were accustomed to using a meal as drivers use gas stations—just for intake. After that, it's on your way. At first I didn't realize how much difference my own presence would make.

With family groups, I had often worked over the theme, "There's no fighting around food." But that wasn't the problem. The need was sharing, having enough interest in others to be together a little while. We would pray and eat. Then there would be a nervous lull. I'd become a kind

137

of master of ceremonies—a poor man's Johnny Carson. But once I'd begun, the men would start to pull out stories and the laughter flowed.

This experience of living in a small group together impressed me so much that, come late August, I couldn't tell the men, "It's been charming, but the students are coming back. You'll have to leave." I just couldn't turn them out on the street again. We begged, borrowed, and hurried, and by September I'd found another house. The whole family of men moved together into a new home. The first one had been called "Maria House." The name came from a visit the students made to the Trappists at Gethsemani, where a monk gave them a painting of Mary. When we moved out, we took the name Maria House with us.

Strangely, I had the notion that the family would be permanent. The first time a man left, I was shocked. I felt cheated, as if the Lord had entrusted him to me and I had failed, or Christ had failed. If someone started drinking again, my stomach would tighten up. I'd go from bar to bar to bring him back alive. With much prayer and thought I grew beyond that, taking a broader view of the providence of God and occasionally glimpsing the good things that resulted from our having shared life for even a little while. So I came to share life with some of the most colorful characters I've ever known.

∞

I had been acquainted with Blackie Sullivan for years. He had a drinking career that was older than I was. Almost always, though, he'd taken care of himself. He was utterly disgusted with anyone who got an assistance check or Social Security check and drank it up without paying rent. His wisdom was basic. Pay for the room and food first. Then drink.

He was one of my friends from Suicide Park, one of the first I met after I knew Rusty. Shortly after I was ordained, when he was sleeping in an alley near lower State Street, he was doused with gasoline and set on fire by some youngsters looking for excitement. He was rushed to the hospital, and amazingly he survived. For months he was hanging almost like a side of beef, his body raw, skinless, susceptible to any kind of infection. I was able to anoint him, but when I visited, I had to talk to him from the doorway. Once as I was leaving, I just shook my head—at the dreadful pain of the whole pointless thing.

He thought I'd given up on him and was frightened. He called the nurse, who treated him with a gentleness that amazed me. He called her "Red." If love and care brought him through it, it was because of Red.

When Blackie got out of the hospital and came back into town he couldn't quite make it on his own. So he asked—and that wasn't easy for him—if he could come to Maria House. He could.

When he was settled in, he said he'd never been able to have a kitten, could he have a kitten. The group in the house thought it was a great idea, so Blackie and I went up to the humane society, where he picked out a little grey kitten with tiger stripes. He called it "Cisco," and he loved it. The bond that grew between them was my first glimpse of how effectively animals can be involved in therapy.

One day when Terry Staff was taking out the garbage, he found a little black and white kitten. When he brought the kitten in, I could feel the tension; the new cat was an intruder—a threat to Blackie. But once the kittens began playing happily together, Blackie and the men approved the new cat.

Blackie was stubborn—probably a reason he was still alive—and had deeply ingrained prejudices. His father, a Chicago detective, had been killed by a black man. Two of the boys who set fire to him were black. When Gus Hicks visited me at Maria House, Blackie went into a huff. Did Gus want to move in, and if so, would he have a vote? I argued with Blackie many times about his prejudice, his need to forgive, and he'd pull age on me. He knew if I lived longer and weren't so protected, I'd agree with him.

Three weeks later at a house meeting, we were discussing Cisco, and somebody spoke about "the other cat."

I said, "What do you mean?"

He said, "You know, that other cat."

After three weeks, the "garbage cat" had no name. As we tried to figure out why, "the new cat" became the symbol of every new person who came. And they came more often. If somebody that we don't know comes, we don't know his name or her name. That person isn't quite real. Distanced, not quite human.

"Doesn't it bother you," I asked one time, "if you don't know the names of people around you?"

"No, I know the people that are important to me."

"Well, what about the other cat that came out of the garbage?"

"Well, he's a garbage cat, obviously."

To welcome the people who came, as human, we had to start with a name. Jesus said, "I call you by name."

The skin that was grafted over Blackie's burns contracted unevenly and caused him much pain. He used Darvon for relief, but it was addictive and diminishing in effectiveness. Blackie would go on an occasional drunk. He couldn't drink for long and always became violently ill. When we were trying to help him out of his hangover, he'd say,

"I learned my lesson this time."

And I'd say, "I hope so, Blackie." Though I knew that in his seventies, he was learning a lesson he'd learned hundreds of times before. When he was in trouble, he always wanted someone to take care of Cisco for him; when he came back, I knew he was feeling better when he'd reach out for Cisco and fall asleep in a rocker with Cisco on his lap.

One afternoon an elderly woman who had a birdbath in her backyard came to the house with fire in her eyes. Several birds had been killed in her backyard by a cat, and she described Cisco. Blackie answered the door. Surprisingly, he wasn't hostile; he heard her out. Then he said, "That sounds like the Father's cat, you'll have to talk to him about it. I'll tell him you were here." That's the only time he ever referred to the cat as mine. After we had Cisco neutered, he stayed at home. Blackie and Cisco mellowed together.

We acquired another house, and more residents.

Terry Staff was about forty when I met him. Some students were staging a moratorium in Perry Square and had asked me to talk on the morality of war. As I talked, I saw the students were not especially interested in the morality of war, but Terry, who had been drinking, stood in the back of the crowd, smiling broadly, and nodding in approval. As soon as I finished speaking, he came up to give me a silver dollar, which he said he had had for years. Terry was a veteran, a pilot. He told me he had watched me often as I walked through the park and he knew Jesus approved of what I was doing. Then he was gone.

Weeks later, I had a call from a hospital that Terry was being released from the alcoholic ward. He was in a wheelchair, with no place to go. When I picked him up at the hospital, they handed me an abbreviated chart. Basic facts, and the words, "Prognosis, dismal."

Terry had a gift of sensing quickly anything phony. That made it hard for him to live in America. Many times, when he'd meet a visitor of mine—a priest, a teacher, a lawyer, a business man—in no time he could lay his finger on weaknesses that it would take me much longer to recognize. But he carried within himself a notion that if he were loyal to the Spirit for awhile, he had a right to some partying. Every time he went drinking he got in trouble.

One St. Patrick's Day, he dyed himself green and went joyfully from bar to bar. He wound up in a rather tough cafe where there were a number of blacks. There he gave them a lecture. He said if they thought it was hard to get along in Erie because they were black, they ought to be green for awhile. That was another fight. Once, when he'd been sober for quite a while, he bought a car. Then he started to drink, was in a wreck, and wound up in traction. That kind of thing had happened so often that most of the major bones in his body had been broken. As I was going to the hospital, I had the car radio on. The program included a McDonald's commercial. When I came into the room and saw that he wasn't in great pain, I said, "Terry, on the way over here, I heard them singing your song, 'You deserve a break today.'" He didn't want to hear it.

Occasionally, one of the younger men would get into drugs. That was a whole new field for me—I needed a crash course. The older residents had no tolerance for drug users. In terms of prejudice and self-defense, almost everyone maintains at least one area of virginity. It's usually something that's never been a real temptation to him; but anyone who wanders into that field is despicable—whether it's not paying rent out of his check before he starts drinking, or shooting up. The pure alcoholics could defend themselves by saying, "At least I never monkeyed with drugs." While I was reading about drugs, I was learning by experience.

One afternoon two of the fellows were quarreling about what had happened to some pills, and as I walked in, one was going toward the other with an upraised meat cleaver. I stepped in between them. Dan, who had the cleaver, said,

"Get out of the way, Father. Being a priest isn't going to protect you."

I said, "I'm not moving, Dan. Put down the cleaver."

The other fellow ducked out of the room. Dan's rage turned on me. He threw the cleaver—it lodged in the wall right above my shoulder.

Two other times in that same week, I wrestled to the ground men who were younger and stronger than I. I honestly had no fear. I just knew that I couldn't let one man maim another with a cleaver. Since Christ called me to the work, he was responsible—and would be protective in ways that were more than adequate. But I had to remind myself often that my neighbors and friends shared neither those experiences nor that confidence.

∽

One Sunday morning, I awakened early with the springtime sun playing about the room. I remembered that it was Pentecost and felt glad. The feast of the coming of the Holy Spirit meant much to me and always carried fringe benefits that made it special. That morning I was looking forward to a late Mass out at the Benedictine convent and I wanted to meditate on the readings in quiet.

The sounds of an argument drifted up the stairs—two of the residents who were returning drunk. I had learned that to be hostile or demanding to people who are drunk simply makes matters worse, but I didn't want them to disturb the whole house, so I went down to get them quiet. Terry was one of them; since he felt he had a right to some partying again, he didn't feel guilty. Besides that, he knew it was Pentecost. He said, "Can I go to church with you this morning?" Since trying to convince him he was drunk would have been pointless, I told him I couldn't take him because I was going to a convent. He wasn't resentful; he just didn't want to go to a parish church where the people would be well dressed and in a hurry and concerned too much about money and not care enough about God or about really hurting people. Then he and Frank Miller, who was with him, said that people need more of the gospel. They had been preaching it in a bar for most of the night.

Terry knew I was concerned about the noise. He said, "Don't worry, Father; I know I shouldn't be drinkin' or preachin', but I know you mean what you preach. I know us guys give you a lot of trouble. But this is only the beginning. Wait till the multitudes come. You wait till the multitudes come. You're really gonna' need people to help." He and Frank said they would change clothes and help. Then they went upstairs. I wondered where to look for the fringe benefits of Pentecost. In the few minutes of quiet I opened to the reading for that Sunday. Peter, in the Acts of the Apostles, began by saying,

"These men are not drunk as you suppose; it is only nine o'clock in the morning." And I smiled. Especially since it was only nine, I wouldn't be late for Mass.

A few Sundays later, I was celebrating Mass again at the Benedictine convent. As I was beginning the sermon Terry came into the chapel, more than a little high. Some of the older sisters were a bit frightened, and I didn't want a scene, but I wasn't sure how to handle the situation, so I just went on preaching. Terry walked right on up to the sanctuary listening intently, not saying a word. He came over to the lectern, which was a bit elevated and knelt on the step. Then he reached his hand up to me and asked a question about whether God could ever love him after he had done such lousy things, whether God could love him as he loved the sisters. I answered very gently, knowing how easily Terry would pick up the vibes of fear or rejection. We carried on a dialogue for possibly three minutes. It was a vignette so beautiful that in being staged it would have been utterly maudlin. As it actually unfolded, it was a moving statement of the great mercy of God, of the power of the sisters' prayer and the beauty of working with broken people. Terry was at peace. He went easily with one of the sisters to get coffee while the rest of us went on with the Mass.

Not long after that, I was having an evening Mass with the Sisters of Mercy. As I started the homily, Terry came into the chapel. Inwardly, I groaned, prayed briefly—"Lord, you take care of it"—and went on preaching. He kept coming forward, but then leaning on a pew, he genuflected, and didn't get up. All through the Mass he was kneeling there with his arms and his head resting on the pew. As soon as I went into the sacristy, a sister came in. "There is a man out in the chapel who is unconscious. I think he might be a friend of yours." I told her I thought so. Then I went and woke him up and took him home—and thanked God.

Small group living was going so well that we had two houses now, and a number of friends helping to keep the houses human. But if there were a problem in either house when I wasn't there, none of the residents could tell me about it without being a snitch. I'd come into a house where the tension was palpable. No one would dare explain why, but since I had the authority I was the warden, and everyone expected me to solve it. My problem with Terry and with a number of others was how to handle them if they fell back into drugs or alcohol. Rules are easily made. No drugs or alcohol in the house; no coming to the house under the influence of drugs or alcohol. But if a man violated the rules and I barred him from our houses, I was cutting him off from the few friends he had, from the one possible avenue he saw to dignity. Beyond that lay the further problem of friendship. That was easy. My concern was not primarily for "a program." It simply never entered my mind that my friendship could be provisional, that failure in the program would end it.

I began to think of a place in the country to get away from drug traffic, from bars and state stores. Then if I had to ban someone from the Maria Houses, I could take him to a safer place where he could develop some before he came back. That way he wouldn't feel rejected. There would still be hope. With a few friends I found a farm near Findley Lake, which the owner was willing to rent for a year. It was on a remote dirt road, had a great deal of room for planting, a few sheds, a rugged woods, and a meandering stream that spoke endlessly of peace. It became Meditation Brook Farm.

∽

For celebrating Mass and teaching, and an appointment with the bishop, I'd change out of my jeans and clodhoppers. When Doug Kennedy asked whether we could get some pigs, I had on my marrying-and-burying shoes; I was on my way to an appointment with Bishop Watson. When we finished our business, he asked how things were going. I explained Meditation Brook to him. Then I asked whether he'd buy four pigs for us. He paused. No one had ever asked him for four pigs. Then he agreed, and in two days we were in the pig business. Doug treated the pigs as pets. If he was a bit down, he'd take a folding chair out to the pig pen and talk to them for an hour at a time.

We also acquired a beef cow that was due to freshen, and a striking red and white horse. The horse was so stately, the fellows named him "Lordship." Then we found a small herd of sheep, a ram and seven ewes.

What happened amazed me. My desire had been to get away, but I had come to something beautiful. One twenty-two-year-old had no trouble with the law, but his whole life had gotten messed up in Vietnam. He couldn't handle work; he cared little for himself; he couldn't stand living with his family. They thought he was lazy; they didn't want to put him out but they weren't able to help him; and his being at home seemed very harmful to his younger brothers. He came for a week to see whether he could fit. That was the week Lordship arrived, and that was the week that light came back into his eyes. When I asked him to take responsibility for the care of Lordship, he jumped at the chance. He groomed him and befriended him, and in four months his own inner energy and his self-confidence had returned.

The men from big cities often carried with them an attitude of superiority and cynicism. *They* knew the world; it was cruel. The animals helped much to change that. You realize there's a great deal of the world you've neither experienced nor conquered when you don't know which end of a cow to milk or what to do to have a sheep bred. If pigs need a man for water or food, he is important. He cannot simply shrug his shoulders and say, "Nothing means anything."

Once when I was away, a neighbor who'd been helping the guys understand the care of sheep brought a case of beer to the farm in a neighborly gesture that almost tore the place apart. When I arrived, the men were all gone, a huge picture window was broken, the living room was a mess. I found them around a bonfire out in the woods, finishing the beer and wanting more.

By morning everything had quieted down, but I was exhausted, utterly incapable of sleep. I went to be sure the sheep were all right, fed the pigs, watered Lordship. Then I noticed the cow was missing. I was tired and discouraged, but I was afraid someone had let her out of the pasture and that she might be a hazard on the road. The morning was very foggy, so a car could come upon her without warning. I walked down into the pasture. There she stood with the fog rising around her like a ghostly landscape, and there at her feet was a beautiful newborn calf. The mother didn't want me to come close, so I didn't. But my heart memorized the scene. I can still find the assurance that it brought if I look into my heart. Sometimes I need to look.

∽

Even with all the pressure, great things happened at the farm that year. We decided now to buy, rather than rent, a farm. With the help of family and friends, Maria House Projects was now organized as a nonprofit organization. We found a rolling piece of land with a large house, a barn, woods, a good-sized stream, and forty tillable acres. Ninety-eight acres, miles from nowhere. Our bid was accepted, and we were in possession of Martha's Farm. I was doing a good deal of traveling—to and from the college in Erie where I was still teaching, preaching at Rockview prison, and managing the two farms.

One Sunday I had Mass at Meditation Brook Farm in the late morning and was driving to Martha's Farm for an afternoon Mass, when I realized I hadn't brought any wine with me. I hoped earnestly there would be none at Martha's Farm, but I knew I would need some for Mass. I stopped at a little hotel bar in Wattsburg to see whether I could buy some wine. I was in jeans, but I explained that I was a priest and needed some wine to take with me. The bartender said it was illegal for him to sell any alcohol to go outside the premises, then he looked at one of the customers and said,

"Now I've heard everything. No one ever tried that before."

A woman in the bar recognized me and said, "Why that's Father Peterson."

He asked her, "Where's he pastor?"

She thought for only a second, and said "Oh, he's in business for himself."

Quietly I got the wine.

Thanks be to God, it was the only wine at the farm when I arrived.

It was a hard winter. We decided to move the animals from Meditation Brook to Martha's Farm. The sheep, the cattle, the horse went easily. But when Doug Kennedy, Mike Phillips, and I were all ready to go, the pigs were not about to move. We tied one with ropes and it dug into the snow and pulled away. We tried pulling them in the direction we didn't want them to go, hoping they'd pull against us and we could let them win. But that didn't work. *We* did. We worked. We froze. We pulled. Finally, kicking and squealing, the pigs came to Martha's Farm, and we were at home.

For the next year I slept at Martha's Farm, drove the forty miles to Gannon to teach and returned in the evening. The first summer I spent at the farm there were fourteen men there. In wintertime that would be far too many, but the men were busy outside in the summer. There was much to do. I was trying to figure our common denominator. Not all the men were alcoholics; not all were drug addicts; not all were ex-convicts. As I thought about it, I realized that the only thing they had in common beyond their humanity and their brokenness was that they were all veterans. Then it struck me what a tremendous impact the wars had had psychologically on each of them. I knew that what we were about was not only some controlling of addiction but a healing of memories and the nurturing of an interior hope that would make the handling of this world's hassles not too high a price to pay for what was accomplished.

I'd enjoyed every one of my years at Gannon College: every class, every counseling session. But I'd heard myself repeating, "Every year the freshmen are getting younger." Partially, that had always seemed so. It annoyed me that some other faculty members referred to the students as "kids." Certainly many of them came burdened with almost unbelievable immaturity. What happened to them in a year's time, though, was not a kid's game; they learned to face some very basic decisions about their faith, their identity, their hopes, and their responsibilities. It was a great privilege to have their confidence, to be a friend and a sounding board, and often to praise God, to whom each one was important. When they left in June, part of me went with them. The new freshmen always seemed much younger by comparison.

I was getting older. I wasn't just a big brother, or an uncle or a kind father. I was a bit grandfatherly. I was convinced that I should be working full-time with older people. My first thought was to try to work full-time with Maria House Projects, to live at Martha's Farm and work with prisons, rehab centers, and our own houses. Only I couldn't imagine life without the liturgy; going without Mass on any day would be like failing to get dressed.

One day the priests of the diocese received word that the parish of St. Teresa of Avila in Union City would be in need of a new pastor. Martha's Farm was in the parish of St. Teresa of Avila in Union City, one of the poorest areas of the diocese. There was little industry; there were many people on public assistance. From being prison chaplain in Erie I knew that they had a high percentage of active alcoholics and, for a very small town, an alarming drug problem.

But it had been in the rectory of St. Teresa's in Union City that my grandmother married William Peterson. It was to Union City that she walked with her children and only the clothes they could wear and carry. And where she did laundry for fifty cents a day. My dad and his sisters had been baptized there; my great grandparents were buried there; and Martha's Farm was in the parish.

In prayer, I felt much at peace—as if "For this I was born."

13

Back to Union City

NOT LONG AFTER I CAME TO THE PARISH IN UNION CITY, A LITTLE child wandered from his home and was drowned in a neighbor's pond. I stopped to see the parents, who were not active parishioners. They were very poor and, of course, utterly crushed. Several times I visited and prayed with them. Although they wanted no penalties, they were insistent that the owner of the pond should put a fence around it so that it wouldn't be a hazard for another child. The owner was adamantly against it. It was his property. It was out in the country. No one could tell him what to do. With all the sadness, I dreaded a possible legal action, so I went to see the man who owned the pond—a veteran named Carl.

He was defensive. I listened. After a while he asked questions about my attitude toward Union City. He knew of some of my relatives there. Then we talked of the pond and the child and the future, and he agreed that he would put up a fence and told me that I could assure the family he would. I knew from even one discussion that he was a man of his word, so I conveyed it.

Carl and I became friends. Whenever I stopped, we'd pray together. Once he took me into his confidence about the town. He said, "You know, I've watched you and admired you, but you don't know what you're doing. You don't realize what a tough problem you have. Union City is a wood town, and it doesn't take a great deal of intelligence to work in wood. So

the pay isn't very much. Anyone with any intelligence who wants to provide for his family goes somewhere else to make a living. The ones who
stay are not too smart. They marry the ones who stay, and you're working with their children." He was saying I was working with a genetic problem. In some measure, he was right, but they were my people—not just
those who were baptized as Catholics but Christians belonging to other
denominations as well, and not just the churchgoers but all the
unchurched, the unbaptized, the unwashed. We were part of one family.

The three-story brick building serving as St. Teresa's rectory was one
of the finest homes in the city. Money to build it had been raised by very
poor people soliciting help from very poor people. At the time of its con-
struction, the immigrant people were making a statement that they could
do what WASPS had done, that they were past shanties and shacks. But
now Union City was one of the poorest areas of Erie County. I had no
need of all that room, and I couldn't live in a palace and bring Christ to
the poor. It started me thinking.

I asked at a parish senate meeting whether I could use the rectory for
people in need and received a ready assent. I had no particular plans in
mind. It's just when I receive something, I like to share it. As a parish we
decided that we were Christ's Church; he was sending us not only to
those who were baptized Catholics—active or inactive—but to all people.
I liked that. It meant that as pastor I did not belong only to the Catholics-
who-are-regular-in-attendance; I belonged to Christ and to all the people
of the area. And they belonged to me.

Then I wondered about those who wandered into the area—roadmen,
returning ex-convicts. Union City was a small town with no shelters. After
a few months, there were several elderly men living in the rectory who
had no one to share life with, who couldn't afford a home for the aged.
One of the first was George McIntosh, a veteran, who had not had a home
since the death of his wife, Mary. He had been in and out of veterans' hospitals for years and at one time had had a very serious drinking problem.
For a while he lived at Maria House in Erie. He was precise in his dress
and manner, a high Episcopalian in fact and in attitude, but unable to
make it on his own. Living at the rectory delighted him. George became

a very prim part of the parish Golden Age club. He was one of the few who came who was at ease with the parishioners almost from the start.

In the hospital, I met a young man who had been in a motorcycle wreck. It turned out that Rick was a high school dropout and was living alone in a trailer in the country without any utilities. When we talked about finishing high school, he was agreeable, but didn't see how it was possible. I invited him to live at the rectory, with the one condition that he finish high school. He had a light sense of humor and did much to help with George and the others. After he was there for a few months, he asked whether he could have a dog. He could if he would housebreak it and care for it. That he did most responsibly, and Rascal became part of our family.

George's father had taught his children that it wasn't right to have an animal in a room where you were eating. Dad never taught us that, but I was the last one in the world to tell George his dad was wrong. So Rascal stayed out in the kitchen while we were eating, at least when we heard George's voice. I figured that if my Uncle Con's dog Shep could learn a whole herd, so could Rascal.

Harry Leed was a parishioner who was living alone on Miles Street. He was a widower, almost entirely crippled by arthritis. I worried about him when I took him communion. Once when he was confined to bed and was worried about the whole future, I asked him to come to the rectory. It had never entered his mind that such a thing was possible. At the time, Doug Kennedy, a powerful young man who handled the pony on Palm Sunday and built the stable when it was needed at Bethlehem, was staying at the rectory. Powerful as he was, he was orderly, gentle, and strong in faith. On a very cold day, he went over to Miles Street, wrapped Harry in blankets and brought him home to the rectory. Sometimes he ate in his room. Many times, he came to eat with us, and then he shined. Even when he was very sick and weak, he did not want to go to the hospital. Finally, I insisted, but he died two hours after he was admitted.

About once a week I'd get into Erie. Regularly, I'd stop to see Rusty— we'd remained friends over the years since those early days when he first came to my office from Suicide Park. His leg was weaker and he was living upstairs in the Kenyan Hotel. Because of the stairs and the slippery sidewalks, he found it hard to shop, so I'd get groceries for him. But he wouldn't even consider moving to Union City. It was too far from the park where his friends were.

Then he had a stroke. In the hospital I told him I was going to take him to the rectory to recover. I didn't ask him; I told him. He was very stubborn, but in the right circumstances so am I. He came and was conquered. His speech never came back completely. By the time he came, Mary Samick had come as housekeeper and cook. Often her children, Chris and Becky, ate at the rectory. Rusty loved them. Mary was very good to him, to all the men. Rusty loved to be with the children, to listen to them laugh. He lived there for about five years. Everything in the parish was important to him. Everything I did was important, though he would never let me cook for him. Others could. I thought it was a matter of respect, but I knew deep down that my cooking was lousy. Toward the end, he became very weak, but he would not go to the hospital. This time, I was not stubborn. He died at the rectory, quietly in the middle of the night.

∞

A few weeks before I became pastor, I was helping at Martha's Farm. One day as I started to lift some wood, my hand went limp; when I tried to move, I fell; and I could feel my face becoming contorted. I thought I was having a stroke. The first thought that entered my mind was that I didn't have to finish piling the wood. After all kinds of tests the doctor told me I wasn't sick, just old. I knew I had to do less. I found that I needed a nap daily. After resisting it briefly, I found that I enjoyed it. If I skip it, my condition later in the day reinforces the doctor's prescription. A man has what is given him from heaven. It is enjoyable to have a nap as part of the allotment.

My fear that I would wind up as one of those old-time pastors who ran a one-man show was long gone. I knew my limits, and I had seen the damage that is done by failing to live as a true community, truly sharing in the work. The decision to include others was our decision. In the change of climate about sisters being confined to the tyranny of pastors—a climate I'd battled with little success years earlier—one by one several sisters came to join the work.

Sister Ignatius Schlaak, who had a brother who was an invalid in the parish, joined our community to work with the elderly, with teaching, with prayer groups, with the work of sacristan. Then Sister Maria O'Connor, a Mercy Sister who had taught for years in college, came to direct the education program and build community in the parish through taking time to know many people individually. Sister Jennifer Pianta, a Sister of St. Joseph and teacher of social work, came. I had lived to see the rigid definitions of priest, sister, layman, and laywoman gradually give way to the appreciation of each individual's gifts. Together in the parish we shaped a new community—in directions I as pastor would not have taken alone. Little by little, we were becoming a healing community.

As one or another person would wander into Union City, sometimes the police would call, sometimes the hospital. With the release of a large number of patients from mental hospitals, communities were not prepared to receive them. Often I'd provide transportation to a rehab center or, for the men, a bed at the rectory. But I was much troubled by the lack of a shelter for the women.

Sister Jennifer, through her work with social services at the hospital, had contacted various agencies to obtain utilities, food, and clothing. She helped put together Horizon House for battered women. When the Thomas More Club disbanded at Gannon, the members turned over Maria House to me for my work, and another sister, Sister Marilyn Zimmer, set it up as a home for women.

∽

Sometimes in winter, a heavily bundled traveler would come to the door of the rectory, all frosted with snow. He would say he was referred by someone at the diner to come there for food. If it was near dinnertime, I'd invite him to come in and let him know we'd be eating in a little while. He'd be surprised, pleased. Then he would ask whether there was a place where he could spend the night. When I said we had an extra bed and he'd be welcome to it, he'd show great relief. Then he'd wonder if there was any chance he could use a washer and dryer. A yes to that would bring him even more serenity. If I'd ask him to stay for a few days to rest up or to wait for the storm to pass, he would be a picture of comfort and ease. All his problems were solved.

Within a day he'd become a nervous wreck, because he didn't know what to do with his mind. As a road man, he would be on his way early in the morning. By noon he'd be wondering, "Where can I eat? Where can I get in out of the weather? Where will I sleep?" As each one of his problems was solved, he would have a minor triumph. The sum of them would make his day. Deprived of those concerns, he was at a loss.

It came to me that the road is an addiction—as much as alcohol, or gambling, or drugs. It also came to me that many roadmen and women, many homeless people have difficult mental problems, painful social problems. People out of mental hospitals, ex-convicts who do not belong—they need more than a house and a job. To me, they were part of my people.

St. Francis of Assisi, whose great mission from Christ was to renew his Church, thought at first of redoing buildings with new stones and mortar. In the Church of St. Damien, Jesus had spoken to him from a crucifix. In obedience he started to build. In loyalty, he started to understand. The rebuilding was a matter of living stones. The body of Christ had many parts. The head could not say to the feet, "I have no need of you." And the merchant could not say to the beggar, "I have no need of you." Francis knew all people were his, but he knew deep within himself a fear of lepers. He hoped he had no need of them. When it entered his mind that Christ might want him to accept them, he dismissed the notion as unthinkable.

Then he met a leper coming toward him in a place too narrow to avoid. He wanted to run, but when their eyes met, the leper's eyes were like the eyes of Christ on the cross of St. Damien. He embraced him, he kissed him, and he was free.

It always worried me when people regarded the poor as a hobby of mine—often enough, as a hobby they wished I would give up for golf. But if a Christian community establishes its identity apart from the poor and the broken, they say, "We have no need of you." The community then is artificial. In the measure the community is distorted, each member is distorted. Each priest is incomplete—not only legally or socially, but emotionally and spiritually. The Church, wherever it exists, is to be the community of God's people. It is not enough to have a gathering for celebration, a Eucharist that belongs to only a part, with the poor gazing in, their noses pressed against the windows, their loneliness wishing to belong anywhere. Or they may no longer look toward the assembly. In their rejection, they lie along the road or the streets.

God told Nathan to tell David, "I have never dwelt in a house, from the time when I led Israel onward, even to this day, but I have been lodging in tent or pavilion as long as I have wandered about with all Israel. Did I ever say a word to any of the judges of Israel whom I commanded to guide my people, such as 'Why have you not built me a house of cedar?'"

It is wonderful to me that our century embraced Mother Teresa, as she embraced the dying, the hopeless, and insisted on the holiness of God and the holiness of each human being made in the likeness of God.

∞

The first year I was at St. Teresa's we had twin lambs born at Martha's Farm the day before Christmas Eve. That was surprising to me. Almost always they are born in the spring. I took them for the children's Mass and passed them around the church so the children could feel them. The lambs were too young to take outside, but at the end of Mass the children formed a procession—including a pony on which Mary rode with Joseph walking next to her. Then we went as a group to an outdoor stable with a live heifer and full-grown sheep and a manger, in which the Child Jesus was placed. Then we all sang Happy Birthday to Jesus.

For the children's Mass on Easter, we asked children to bring baskets and gave them a colored egg and another gift—possibly a homemade butterfly. We had them rehearse an Easter message, so that as they gave the basket to a parishioner sick at home, or a grandparent, or a neighbor they carried the message to. Ordinarily around the baptismal font we had live baby chicks, or ducks, or rabbits, and a lamb or two. Many people had warned me about the danger to lambs of letting people deal too much with them. They said it could easily happen that the lamb would be rejected by its mother—a high price to pay for a visual aid. But we never had a lamb rejected.

Always I used the animals and chicks as part of the homily, and always they cooperated. A duckling at the microphone is a real ham. When the organ played, the chicks peeped more loudly. And when the children came forward to sing a song, all the congregation was happy. Their minds are so beautiful. Little Stephanie Hakel, when she was three, decided she wanted to get married and wanted me to be celebrant in the wedding. But she wasn't going to leave me; she invited me to ride along "on the front of their honeymoon." I told her I wished she could always be three. But she outgrew it. That's the way things go.

Not only the feasts and weddings and funerals, but every Sunday every celebration was new. I love the liturgy. On any Sunday, the Lord wants us to taste Easter; and I tasted Easter there and wondered each time how many more times it could happen.

∞

One morning I got a call from Dr. Zoltan Heya at St. Vincent's Hospital. We had been at Gannon together. He was the finest portrait painter I have ever known, a learned man, a man of faith. When he called, he was flustered. He hated to inconvenience me by asking me to make a special trip, but he would appreciate it if I'd stop sometime when I was in Erie. I knew he was a very private person and that the call was not easy, so I went that afternoon.

He was in a special unit. He had had surgery several times for cancer. The doctor had just told him that he needed another operation. He asked the doctor what the operation would achieve and whether he would be able to leave the hospital, to paint, to do anything. The doctor said all those things were unlikely, but it might prolong his life by several months. He saw no reason to prolong his life at such a cost. He was not able to do any good; the expenses were spiraling. Soon they would eat up everything he had saved, money that he wanted to leave for his daughter and granddaughter. I assured him that they would care little about the money, but I also told him he was not bound to take such unusual means to prolong his life, that morally he was not bound to the operation he described. He said that was the only thing he was inquiring about. He wanted to be sure he was doing nothing wrong in refusing the operation. As I reassured him, he said, "Well, that's what I will do. Next time he comes, I'm going to tell the doctor, but he's going to be very angry."

"He may be, Doc. But it's your life."

The following week when I stopped, he was smiling. He had just received communion. He said, "Remember what I told you about the doctor? He wasn't upset. When I told him I was not going to permit the operation, he looked right into my eyes and said, 'You know, you have a lot of common sense.'"

Three weeks later I was celebrant at his funeral.

Parish life brought me close to many elderly people facing prolonged illness at the end of life and gave me a deepening sense of what the sacramental life means as a man or a woman faces death.

Several women in the parish whose husbands were bedridden or crippled were actually operating one-woman intensive care units in their own homes. This was not just a moment of heroism; it was a constant way of life. A restricting life. Yet there was no fuss, no fanfare, no complaints. They were so grateful anytime I came; I was humbled by the quiet with which they loved one another.

We began having an annual anointing Mass. In the early days of my priesthood the sacrament of the anointing of the sick was saved for the moment before death. Extreme Unction—even to mention it often stirred panic. The old people became accustomed to the new rite of anointing, involving a prayer of healing—physically and spiritually. Many came by car for our anointing Mass, many with relatives. Some came by ambulance. It was beautiful when, as a group, we looked death in the eye, and death flinched.

I've always had a great love for the Eucharist. Taking communion to the elderly who were sick deepened it further. Several times I saw people who were disoriented suddenly focus their attention when I held up the host. At first I thought it was a coincidence, but repeatedly I saw the coming of a peace that could only be the product of a living faith. These people had no sophisticated theology of sacramental life. In two instances they were illiterate. In the case of Polish and Slovaks, we were separated by language, but when I held up the Eucharist, each one knew and responded.

One day at the hospital, after I had prayed with one of our own parishioners, another patient in the same room asked me if I had time to talk. I did. He said his name was Clair Cook. He didn't want to seem insolent, but he couldn't see anything wrong with suicide, and he supposed I disagreed with that viewpoint. Would I explain why?

I spoke of the sovereignty of God and of the inalienable right of life, which rested in our duty to grow in his love. If people refuse to suffer, they refuse to grow. I spoke of trust. If not a bird falls from heaven but by God's will, then we are in his care. If a person's work is done, God takes him. In the narrow places of our lives, it is dangerous for us to think we are in charge.

That didn't strike him as enough reason to be an inconvenience to the people around us when we can no longer help ourselves. We prayed together, and I left. I saw him several more times. When he left the hospital, he left a note asking me to stop at his home. It was on Hemlock Street, which was still unpaved—much as it had been when Gramma moved into the old Shea House. When I stopped to see him, he said he wanted to be a Catholic.

We had never discussed that, and I told him it was not a package deal. That I could visit him even if he were not a Catholic. He said that wasn't it. He was so edified by the faith of Catholics in receiving communion that he wanted to belong. When he was well enough to get out, he planned to go to the Presbyterian Church, thank them for his years there, and tell them he wanted to take his name off the register and why. The next time I stopped at the house, he said he had gone to church on Sunday, but he just wasn't able to tell them that he was leaving. I told him again that he didn't have to leave. He believed in Christ; he belonged to him. We could pray together and be at peace.

When he was sick, I had anointed him. Now he wanted to know if I could bring him communion. I apologized. I simply could not. He had begun to read scripture and loved the sixth chapter of John—Christ, the bread of life. Next time I was there, he said he couldn't be at ease without the Eucharist. It was a persistent yearning that would not let him alone.

"My mind is made up. Will you receive me into the Catholic Church?"

I told him I would if he was sure it was what he wanted, but it couldn't be provisional. We discussed the sacramental life, the nature of the church, the papacy. After a few meetings he said he was ready. We set a time. As I was leaving, he said,

"Then will I be able to receive communion?"

"Yes."

"And I can't commit suicide?"

"No."

"I'm ready."

I received him into the church. He lived long enough to receive communion three times. Then he died.

At his funeral liturgy, the whole sacramental reality came to life again for me. Again God's providence in dealing with him was so very specific—*"This* is my beloved son."

∞

I had no question in going to St. Teresa's that Jesus was leading me. It was the Lord's will for me that I be pastor there. I went with a clear realization of his promise that he would make us a healing community.

One man whose marriage had broken up, who had once tried to commit suicide by drinking Drano, came to St. Teresa's and stayed for months. He had a great deal of talent, helped with many things. As we tried to chart a future for him, he was tremendously direct. He said he needed more faith, or at least needed to use it more. It was not a remark typical of him. He saw my inquiring look.

"Father, being here with you is the best thing that has happened to me. Wherever you are, there are people. I see poor people from town come here every hour of the day and night. I see road men come in out of the cold, dirty and shaking. That phone goes all the time. Then there's us guys who need you. You don't even have a private room. So I wondered how you keep going. You never get angry, never hide from people, never push them away. Only sometimes I see your hand shaking. You look so tired, I worry about you. Then you go over to church and stay there for an hour. When you come back, you look different. I know you weren't sleeping. And I know its not my imagination. I've seen it too many times. I know you can't be doing this alone. And with my past, I think, 'Who am I that I think I can do anything alone?'"

He was right. I realized that in my life I'd had so many opportunities for retreat, for spiritual exercises that had helped me survive and grow. Over and over I had found that being with people away from the clutter of daily demands, away from the familiar places and patterns, was important in helping them grow, in leading them into the presence of God. I considered retreat work a sharing with people in the re-forming of their thoughts and lives. At a critical time in my own life I had been able to get away for a thirty-day retreat. But where could these people go?

When a veterinarian who owned one of the finest houses in Union City offered his house to me for my work, I began thinking. If you put eight troubled people in a house, you have eight troubled people in a house. I told him I couldn't handle another place as a shelter. More than I needed more space, I needed more people to help bring that space to life. But when I thought of how much the people I knew needed a place to nourish their own inner lives, I decided to accept the house as a place for retreats. So Avila House came into being.

The huge open fireplace burns honestly. Often the snow quiets everything and makes each visitor snug. There may be two or four or five, retreating from the sounds and clamor of the road, or of the rectory, the kitchen, the shop, or a shelter. In the silence we are all together, before God. Sometimes I just suggest a passage of scripture and get out of the way—to allow God to work in the quiet, in the liturgy. Once I asked retreatants to simply spend time watching the fire; I began with a poem written by Jessica Powers on entering the Carmelites:

> The day is ended with the end of Compline
> A bell has sounded as a discipline

> Against all inner and outer din.
> I seek our cell to pray
> Oh soundless spirit.
> Let the Great Silence in my life begin.

There was a time when I thought silence was proper to any seminary that had depth, or to the Trappists or to the Carmelites. Now I know that anyone who wants to live in the spirit of Christ's gospel needs to find quiet as a friend. Moses had his years with the sheep; the apostles had nights under the stars on the sea; John the Baptist had the desert.

Priests, religious, lay people—professionals in healing—are kept from being functionaries only by an honest interior life. What keeps anyone from "using" those who are in need of healing is an awareness of being loved so much that it reflects on the features of the approaching leper. Without that time for quiet, need for quiet, and even the discipline to be quiet, and to receive, it is too easy to find in the broken a means of income, financial or emotional. How sad it is to rip off the least.

Avila House has become a wellspring for the interior life, bringing together the broken and those who help the broken enough to realize that we are all broken and need each other to be made whole.

∞

Living in Union City for ten years did much to bring me to my roots. I like to wander in St. Teresa's cemetery to read the inscriptions of my own relatives, of former pastors, of children that died young and parents that died young, and of others who died old. When it's quiet there, death cannot be proud. Neither can we. Any number of times it's come to me how as a child I had felt sorry for the "old pastor" standing in the wind and the snow. Now, I'm the old pastor.

Often I asked people at funerals to take their children or grandchildren to the cemetery at sometime other than the burial of a relative. The sadness of parting, the tears of loving people can remain a child's most vivid image of death. If Christ has not risen from the dead, we are the most foolish of people. But he is risen.

I have assured many parishioners as they struggle with the approach of death: "Heaven is more beautiful than Union City." I'm sure that's true.

People lean on my faith rather than on my theology. With all that, Union City is a wonderful place to get ready.

When I left St. Teresa's as pastor, I told the people I didn't want any presents. They had always been so good and so generous to me. All I wanted was a grave. I don't know how soon I'll need it. It doesn't matter much. But with the richness of faith I have shared with very ordinary people whose trust made them giants, I will never again sit in the shadow of death.

14

*The Gospel
in Rockview Prison*

SOMETIMES A PERSON IS JOLTED INTO THE REALITY OF PRISON just by a door clanging behind him, when he realizes clearly for the first time that he has no key to get out. Someone else has the key. Someone else is in charge. Even a visitor knows after the clang that he or she is no longer in control.

Inside, the sights and sounds of a different world accumulate gradually. Sometimes it's a steady roar of sounds—metal trays of food on metal tables in a dining area crowded with the noise of too many people. Or in larger and older prisons, the constant sound level in the living area of piled up cages is several decibels too high for any inmate to think clearly or be at peace.

Over the years, images of unhappiness have piled up in my memory. A long line of shivering men moving slowly in the rain of a cold day to a window through which they would get their medication. Some, I imagined, were waiting for medicine for their colds. Or a man completely naked with his arms handcuffed around a pole behind him—so he couldn't hurt himself. Or men on so much thorazine—liquid handcuffs—that they couldn't even find their cells.

At a seminar once I heard Joe Byerley, who was then superintendent of the Western Penitentiary, say that given his budget, the building he had, and the number of inmates, he could not do one thing for the rehabilitation of any of the inmates. There was a time when a warden would go through the prison to make contact with the inmates daily. Then numbers multiplied, guards multiplied, and wardens or superintendents were pressured with decisions and the budget problems of a growth industry.

Last year, several seminarians who went to visit a prison were amazed at the antagonism between the guards and the prisoners. The guards asked them, "Are you on our side or theirs?" Later the inmates asked, "Are you on our side or theirs?"

Over twenty years ago, Monsignor Walsh, chaplain of the State Correctional Institution at Rockview, Pennsylvania, asked me to come and preach a mission to the inmates. I wasn't sure what it would be like, but I wanted to go. And every year since then I have spent a week of October preaching to the men there in preparation for Dismas Day, the second Sunday of the month.

When I first visited Rockview, I liked the rural setting. There were high towers at each corner, with sentries in them constantly. There were large spirals of razor-sharp wiring on top of all the fences. But there were also open spaces of lawn, flower beds, a greenhouse, an operating farm with beef cattle, a forestry camp—and the Chapel of Our Lady of the Mount. The latter was an island of peace which the inmates had helped construct. It became for me a center of prayer and ministry that has modified my life tremendously.

When I helped Oscar McGrew to get ready for execution, it never entered my mind to go to Rockview with him. That whole scene was something distant from Erie and unknown to me. But even then, I thought it was easier to get him ready for his death than for life in prison. It's cruel to tack the label "criminal" on a man or woman for a lifetime—to take away any hope of reconciliation with the community. Often I am torn between whether merely to scream out against the growing prison system or to try to work within it.

The Letter to the Hebrews, after an account of the trials of God's chosen people, admonishes, "Be mindful of prisoners as if you were sharing their imprisonment, and of the ill-treated as if yourselves, for you may yet suffer as they do" (Heb. 13:3). The author describes Abraham, Moses, Gideon, and others as men of faith, men who could "see the invisible."

I didn't need to see the invisible. My prison mail regularly speaks of what is visible, palpable, to the prisoner whose imprisonment I am to share. A sample:

> Well, remember I told you that their hasn't been any stabbings. I seen a guy yesterday get stabbed right in front of me. He got stabbed quite a few times, twice in the face that I know of for sure. We will be getting a new warden. From what I've heard the guards are glad to see him go probably because he gets along with the inmates so good. They been doing a lot of things around here to harass the inmates. The rumor is that they want trouble, so they can lock the jail down. I had a couple of guards that I'm cool with tell me that if there is a riot the state police have orders to shoot to kill. It's because of what happened at Camp Hill. They brought a bunch of state police in this week to show them the layout of the whole prison. I know they only gave us two pieces of toast and a cup of coffee for breakfast yesterday and they never do that. None of these things bother me that much. In fact with the overcrowding you almost got to expect something to happen sooner or later. My Buddy Bingo got out of the hole, and they gave him a single cell status, the shrink said he shouldn't be double but they won't give him a single cell. Their not suppose to go against the doctor's orders, but their doing it. I kind of feel sorry for the guy. He's been so nervous. I try not to get involved in any of the jail house politics, but I'm not blind.

And who are they—these "hardened criminals" who "deserve to be locked up?" Another letter:

> I have no juvenile record. I married upon graduation at the age of 17 and fathered a son. I then went and volunteered for the U.S. Army and subsequently went to Vietnam where I did a tour and was awarded numerous combat medals. I had a difficult time adjusting to U.S. society upon return; thus substance abuse, and incarceration. I did one year at Rockview for possession of marijuana in 1970–71. I stayed drug free and crime free until 1976—misuse of charge cards 2½ to 7 years in Rockview. I was released in 1979. Lastly I was convicted in 1980 for armed robbery (no violence—no one hurt) and received a 10–20 yr. sentence. My time is almost up—2 yrs. left to do.

Then he says he has no place to go when he gets out. "We did the best we could while he was here." Did we? And when he gets out, whose is he? Thinking no one cares, simply because he can't see anybody that cares.

⌒

One evening as I was talking to a man who was doing his first time in prison, I asked him whether he'd like a religious pamphlet. He said he would, and I offered him a stack to choose from. The one on top was entitled, "Your new leisure." Our eyes met. We started to laugh.

But it made me think, what does a person do with great chunks of time and almost no sense of purpose in his day? Growth—in peace, in freedom, in love—is terribly difficult behind bars. The men and women in prison may be rejects from society, but they are dear to God and need to know it. In surrender to God they are like Paul, who spent time in prison. They are like Peter, who after a long night of fishing on his own and catching nothing, hears Jesus say, "Let down your nets." And they are full.

"Lord, depart from me, I am a sinful man." Forever more, I am the man who got drunk the night of the prom and cracked up a car. And Jesus says, "I will make you fishers of men, let down your nets." You. And Peter says, "Depart from me, I am a sinful man." Isaiah asks, "How can I go? *You* are holy, and I have sinned." To Peter the Lord says, "I will make you a fisher of men."

If God loves us too much to waste a minute of our lives, time in prison cannot be a waste. Somehow it has to embody nourishment and growth. I wanted to help the prisoners develop an interior life, to reflect on what they had done, to learn to meditate on the scriptures, to confront themselves, to learn to speak honestly with God.

When I preached my first mission at the Pennsylvania State Correctional Institution at Rockview, I wondered how much of the gospel I could preach, how directly I could accuse, how much I could expect. I was afraid that any confronting might be understood as a nonprisoner talking to prisoners, instead of the accusation of a sinner calling sinners to repent. By the end of the week I knew we had shared the pure gospel, no holds barred. It was an action of grace more forceful than in any other group I had dealt with.

To nourish the inner life of the prisoners, to bring them to meditation and the scriptures and the inner state that permitted the Spirit to work within them, I had to pierce through the defenses. Once again I was searching for images, a language that these men could connect with, that would bring each one to look on the body of Christ—on him whom we have pierced.

At a school initiation rite some years ago, a prank got out of hand, and the boy being initiated said he couldn't get up from the floor. The others laughed, chided, until they realized that the boy's back had been broken. Later, when they saw him trying to navigate the school corridor on crutches, in a cast, a change came over them. They were subdued. They had to look on him whose back had been broken. This is where any honest confronting in prison must begin:

John, who knew the crucifixion first hand, asks us to look at the dying Jesus.

"They will look on the one whom they have pierced." Not "They will look on the one others have pierced." It is the one we have pierced. Not just the Romans. Not just traitorous Judas. We. You and I. You need to look on your sin. You may have tried to become comfortable with your sin, because "everybody does it," or blame your father who was always drunk, or your uncle who raped you. Or you may feel that because you've quit drugs you have a right not to forgive your daughter who lives in your house and never has time to visit you.

Forget all the blaming of others, of lawyers, of judges, and don't try to conceal from yourself your own sinfulness. Until you know your sins are so ugly that they caused the suffering and death of Jesus, you don't know yourself. You do not see clearly. And you cannot be healed.

A drunken driver is thrilled with his handling of a speeding car. Until he must face the broken body of the child he has killed. He looks on those he has killed. Look on the battered body of Christ, whom you have pierced. "I am a remarkable person, not because I am so bad, or others stay out of my way, or because of my hairdo. I have done this. The risen Lord keeps his wounds. He wants you to see them, to see what you have done.

Alone, this realization could be suicidal. But if you lift him up, if without bargaining, you ask forgiveness, make him Lord in your life, you will see that he didn't die "for people." He died for you.

"My Lord and My God. I give you the butt end of my life. I cannot over-come drunkenness and hatred, dishonesty and impurity, of myself. If I need your power for forgiveness, I need it even more today to live as a child of God."

One year at the mission I met a man named Jim Townsend. He'd been sentenced to life in prison for the murder of his wife. After twenty-some years, he received clemency and found on the streets that he could live a legal life, a responsible life, take care of his own apartment, his own bills, his own planning. In prison—at Rockview—he had come through an hon-est conversion which he never wore on his sleeve. But from the strength of that conversion, he found that "making it" in the American Dream was a charade. Pittsburgh, with all its splendors and the glory of them, was not much of a prize to live for. So he entered a religious order, deepened, struggled with himself, and remembered where he had come from.

When I first asked him whether he'd come with me to the annual mis-sion to give a talk to the men at Rockview, he said he didn't know how to preach. So I told him not to worry about it. Just give them a talk. He did. Very directly. What you see is what you get. And they were rapt. So I asked him whether he'd come for a full week the following year. He said he couldn't preach, and I told him not to worry about it. So he came. That's been going on for fifteen years now.

One evening he gave an introductory talk for a penance celebration. With a burly approach, he said, "There are some of you here who say you believe in forgiveness. You may even go to confession tonight and say you're forgiven. Even with that you can go on the rest of your life beat-ing yourself. When you die, you might even go up to Jesus and say, 'Jesus, I'm awful sorry about that rape.' He'll look you right in the eye and say, 'What rape?' Because he said, 'I'll forgive you your sins and I'll remem-ber them no longer' and he meant it."

One evening when Jim Townsend was talking, he explained his day: waking up in his cell, morning preparation, prayer, work, lunch, and so on through the day. His schedule in the friary was about the same as his schedule had been in prison. All that made the difference was the trust that enabled him to live it in obedience to God.

∞

Often during the mission, an inmate would feel drawn, but not know what he wanted. Each one needed the help to look distinctly, quite specifically, at how God was working through the events of his life. Often a man came to me in bewilderment, able to speak only of confusion. One man I remember well wasn't able to stand far enough away from his confusion to describe it. One thing he was certain about: though he had spent years in living irresponsibly, sinfully, he knew he was not ready for confession. I listened without any attempt to summarize his confusion, to speak for him, or to rush him. Finally, I asked him why he thought that whatever he touched became dirty.

Then he told me of his father. They had never been at ease with one another. His father was always on him, never approved of anything he did, never offered to share anything. Then his father came through a religious experience. He knew very clearly that his father wanted reconciliation, but did not know how to go about it. He said he himself didn't know how to go about it either, had no idea what to say; but he was sure if he just reached out his hand, the old man would accept his forgiveness. Only he was too proud to take the initiative. Then it was too late. His father died. Being able to express that opened up all his self-rejection. As he continued to talk, he walked through his confusion. He laid open his soul.

My concern was not only that he could face his guilt but that he could trust in the desire of Christ to carry it for him, that he could accept forgiveness and expect that by the presence of Christ in his life, he could live as a child of God. When he realized that I could glimpse all that had been and still expect so much of him, it was a help to him to try, to hope, to begin again. He then went to confession and expressed himself in an act of contrition.

The sacrament of penance does not end with the confessing of wrongdoing, or with the penance. Its purpose is to effect reconciliation. Though I'd never thought in these terms, I told him that for his penance he should give a sign of peace to his father. He looked at me questioningly, wondering whether I had forgotten that his father was dead. In answer to his eyes, I said,

"Just go into chapel and close your eyes. In his knowledge of God, your father will know what is happening. Then reach out your hand to him and say, 'The peace of Christ be with you always.' Leave your hand extended until he does the same for you."

He agreed to his penance. I gave him absolution and he left.

The next day I saw him in the entryway to the chapel. The men often gathered there before services. He was talking to a group of his friends, telling them about his reconciliation with his father. He didn't tell them it was part of his penance, but he described the handshake in chapel, the awareness of reunion. And he added, "It was the sweetest, gentlest, most beautiful experience of my life." In prison, a man is taking a chance to describe anything as sweet, beautiful, and gentle. No one grinned; no one attempted humor to help the group out of a tense situation. He was too honest. His soul was too open and vulnerable to risk the slightest bruising.

At Rockview, the annual mission for Catholics ends on Saturday. Later that day, a great many inmates come over to help clean and decorate the chapel. The next day, Sunday, is the feast of St. Dismas, patron of prisoners. Some of the alumni of the place come back; the bishop comes as celebrant and homilist; many friends and families of the inmates come there also.

On this particular Saturday, everything was being washed, moved, dusted, and shined. A young man who had been at several exercises came up to me and said he had dropped out of the retreat because he was afraid he was kidding himself. But he hadn't been able to sleep. Something was pushing him. He wasn't able to get it out of his mind. He knew that at least he wanted to try.

Every office, every room in the building was being cleaned. The only place I could find for privacy was a large broom closet. We took two chairs in, closed the door and sat down. He told the story of his life. That's never easy, but also it's never enough. We were there in Christ's name, and the Christ in the midst of us was at work. Anyone who sins is a slave of sin, but when the Son of Man frees you, you are free indeed. He could confess in a way that enabled Christ to show him himself still alive and breathing under all the weight of his life. And he could look at a future where Christ would be in charge—with or without a good attorney or a sympathetic judge. When he finished, he was young, newborn. I gave him absolution, a handshake of peace, and it was over. Yet neither one of us wanted to leave. There was nothing to say; nothing to teach or learn or add. But we didn't want to stir. It was a moment of communion. Finally, he blurted out, "Y'know, you never think when you go into a broom closet that something like this can happen."

Sure enough, I never thought of it that way.

∞

When I took a trip to Medjugorje, I found that the confessions I heard there involved one marvel of conversion after another in a way that was humbling. "This is God's work; you are a fragile instrument in a moment that touches eternity." The only comparable experience I had ever had was in the October weeks at Rockview—one marvel after another.

In the mission following my visit to Medjugorje, I wondered about speaking of the rosary. There would be a number of men there who were not Catholics, who belonged to other denominations or who were unchurched. To them the rosary would either be unknown or irrelevant or both. "Our Lady" could stir old warnings against idolatry or superstition, which could detract from the central message of the living Christ.

But so many simple people facing harsh lives, with little experience of meditation or reading, found peace in the rosary. So, at one session, I spoke about Mary, and the rosary, and Medjugorje. Afterward, a young man in his twenties asked me if in the next few days I'd have time to say the rosary with him. I'd let him know and we could say it together. It was the first such request I had in prison. I took it seriously.

Two days later when he was coming in, I had some free time. It was lunchtime. The dining room was an uproar of banging tins, of conversations that clashed with one another, of lines of similarly dressed empty faces, or bored faces, or angry faces. It was good to get out of the chaos, back to the quiet of the chapel area. We said the rosary together. It was an experience filled with quiet shared peace, and powerful gentleness. When we finished, we were both at ease and speechless. After a short while, he said, "Wow!" Then he started to laugh. "A lot of good I get from being interested in English, when after a thing like that, all I can say is 'Wow!'"

I know that after the depersonalizing prison, this man needs a healing culture, a redemptive mother. Many of the people I meet have ended up in prison, in mental hospitals, because they were broken by a posthuman world they couldn't cope with. When I visit a home that has video games of which the children have become masters, after I'm whipped soundly several times, I drop the whole thing. "I will not play your game." In the mental wards, in the emergency room where a young woman or man has just been deposited after another try at suicide, I hear the cry, "I will not play your game. It isn't worthwhile. It isn't possible. Why don't you leave me alone? The life I try to endure when I'm incapable of doing anything that anyone needs is empty of meaning. A loving God? Where?"

It seems to me cruel, inhuman, to put a man or woman who has faced with great pain his own actions, come perhaps to a moment of communion—of gentleness that stirs life again—through a ninety-day program when they're released and then drop them back into that same mechanized impersonal world that broke them.

∞

One day a priest whom I knew introduced me to a friend of his, saying that I was on my way to visit the state prison. The man said,

"I hope they're not friends of yours, Father."

I didn't smile. I answered, directly, "Yes. They are friends of mine."

He was taken aback when I didn't laugh at his joke. But to me there was no joking. I have entered into lasting friendships with prisoners, many of them facing long terms. I find among them much honesty and often a faith that embarrasses me. Sometimes when I'm saying Mass it's hard for me to go on. If the men in the choir are singing—and they sing beautifully—I am transfixed. The hymn that speaks to me most of Rockview has a haunting refrain:

> It won't be long and we'll be leaving here;
> It won't be long, we'll be going home.
> Count the years as months,
> Count the months as weeks,

> Count the weeks as days,
> Any day now we'll be going home.

I do not feel detached from them. It's heartrending even to think of the time behind bars before reunion with whatever family remains. It's nearly unbearable when it becomes a longing for heaven. The men sing—and over their humming an inmate recites:

> We shall be like him
> We shall be like him
> For we shall see him as he is,
> Any day now, we'll be going home.

15

Holy Ground

IN THE DAYS WHEN LEPERS HAD TO RING A BELL AND CRY OUT
"Unclean!" the uninfected shrank back from the narrow places in which
they might meet. Many people today view the most broken as lepers. It
seemed to me we needed to shape a community where we can be truly
reconciled—a place and a frame of mind, in which those in the mainstream
and those on the margins of our society might learn to be friends, and
enter a new freedom.

That place is a lovely tract of old farmland in the Pennsylvania hills,
on which the Erie diocese owned a small farmhouse and an old barn. We
call the barn Nazareth. The men have built individual rooms—eight of
them—for themselves, and lined the walls with rough-hewn wood. Here
the road men with no place to go in winter come, and inmates newly
released from prison can adjust to a home without bars, and those recovering from alcohol or drugs or just the confusion of more rejection can
stay a few days, a few weeks, or occasionally a few months while the healing begins. Here they share life with volunteers who are willing to be just
friends.

I love the ride out from Erie several times a week through familiar
hills, often past the cemetery where my grandparents are buried. It's winter now, a couple of weeks after Christmas. As I drive through the snow
up the hill to the converted barn called "The Lodge," a little ritual begins.
Two of the dogs, Lady and Hobo, announce my arrival with constant

barking, then sniff at me, and wait to be petted for doing their work properly. One of the men living here now is riding the tractor, plowing snow.

I slip into the kitchen, give each one there a hug, and go on to the large, open room with the wood pillars and beams and huge stone fireplace. One of the cats is curled up, sleeping near the fire.

Some of the men are full of tattoos. Some of them "look like murderers"; some of them still have the shoes or the earring or the hairstyle that speaks of prison. One may be dejected because of a letter he's had from home—or hasn't had from home. Another asks if I've noticed how he shifted the furniture and cleared away the clutter by the fireplace. One asks if I like the new paint job.

Today, as I often do, I come with visitors and introduce each by name. Today's visitors are women—and I sense a change in the men in the room. It's not just care with language and style—but something more. They know these two women are here simply to be part of the afternoon—to talk, to share a meal, as friends. Broken women need friendship from some males who are caring and gentle. Broken men cannot be whole without this friendship from women, without an experience of women distinct from the harsh stereotypes many have picked up.

The twenty or so of us—residents, visitors, a dog and a cat or two—gather around the fire and read a bit of Luke's Gospel. I learn that the shepherds of Jesus' time were really lower-class. One reason was that they cared for sheep at night. Without flashlights, they'd step on the droppings of the sheep. Then they'd smell bad and others wouldn't want to come close. I don't think it's worthwhile to give a lecture to this group on how different our society has become in making body odor the great sin that renders people incapable of community life. Nasal superiority is a comparatively recent pretension. Since I don't want anyone in the room who has only recently become aware of the importance of taking showers to lose his motivation, I pass by the comment.

We go on to the child. A voice from the beat-up chair on my right asks, "Let's get this straight. *Is Jesus God, or isn't he?*"

The voice belongs to a tough-looking tattooed man, out of prison about a month. I'm quiet for a bit. Others pick up the question—with a surprising reliance on scripture texts.

"The word *was God* and the word *became flesh.*"

And dwelt among us. Pitched his tent next to ours.

Another voice jumps in, "How do ya know that's *love?* And if it *is,* what difference does it make?"

And another, "I never think about this stuff."

Sometimes that comes as an angry statement. Today it isn't. Just honest. "I don't want to pretend." One man with a fundamentalist background injects a passage about the devil, his deceptiveness, his effectiveness in producing offspring or converts as the father of lies.

Old Brother Bernard is here, sitting quietly, listening. He's in his eighties—a Holy Cross brother who gave up his retirement at Notre Dame eight years ago to come and share life with us. He doesn't live at Nazareth, but at St. Joseph's, the old farmhouse across the driveway. Now it has its own chapel and beds for four men with one extra for a guest and no radios or television except for an occasional import when Notre Dame is playing. He doesn't speak much, but when he does everyone listens. When he speaks deeply, his sincerity is palpable. He too has suffered, from joining the brotherhood in an era when the common practice in the Church was to impose a rigid formation. He entered his order as a boy of thirteen. Here he is a living statement of the value of loyalty and the unending power of love.

He speaks of Joseph and Mary as though they were neighboring farmers in Kersey, where he lived before he joined the brothers. He speaks of faith, not cerebral answers to generic problems, but in a way that makes us look into our hearts to see what things are honest and what things are comforting lies; what things are poses and what things are avenues into the hearts of others and into the mind of God.

One man asks him the difference between a brother and a priest, and he quips, "Six dollars a year." He says he's found the most beautiful career of his life at the end of it. When he came a few years ago, Brother wanted the assurance that he could get to Mass every day. And he does. Several days a week he goes to the parish church with men who *want* to accompany him. The other days we share Mass at the lodge. There is never any forcing. I don't want anyone to even have the impression that going to church will gain him points. Some of our men have had very negative experiences of structured religion, congregations full of resentment or of prejudices, city missions where the price of a meal was accepting a great deal of depersonalization and a lengthy sermon before eating.

If anyone asks Brother about his job—it's just to be there. A quiet presence. Working in the garden. Playing the piano. Cooking. Serving a meal to the small group at St. Joseph's. He'll work for hours with a man still smarting from the anger of family rejection and years of imprisonment. He'll tell the ex-convict, eager to help with fresh planting, "It's not hard to get people to work with me to get seeds or plants in the ground. But will you be around when it's time to pull out the weeds or do some watering or some harvesting?" Not just spurts. Continuity. Loyalty. Ripeness is all.

A man fresh from prison a few days ago, quiet until now, asks, timidly, about believing in a loving Father.

"Would it make a difference in how you think about this, if your own father—I mean, if a guy beats his kid a lot, does it make it harder for the kid to stop the violence? I mean, to be a *different* kind of a man—from his father?"

This time I don't hold back. "It sure does." And we're talking now about how hard it is to break that mold, to treat another man kindly, gently, if you've been beaten as a kid. Then we get quiet. And we pray.

Brother jots down a few notes and asks what time we'll have Mass. It's snowing hard now and windy. As Brother hobbles off toward the door at the close of our discussion, one of the men—with a prison earring and a pony tail—notices he's heading into the snowstorm alone. Slipping quietly up beside Brother, he takes an arm, and the two lean into the snow together.

During the afternoon I see most of the men separately. Since many go and come back, and others are here for the first time, sometimes I ask one the name of the man who just arrived a day or two earlier. I'm thinking then of Blackie Sullivan and his cat Cisco, and the "new cat" who didn't have a name.

☙

Once a wanderer from the park was telling me the story of his life. Some of what he described was tragic, some grossly immoral. Whatever he had been discussing, when he was ready to move on, he'd say, "And then I got a '32 Chevy," or "then I got that '30 Studebaker." The pegs on which he hung the story of this life were the cars that he had at the time. They were the transportation by which he came and went from the scenes he remembered, but they also modified his self-image. A different car meant that he approached situations from a different vantage point.

As I think back, the easiest way for me to organize my memories is by recalling the churches, the chapels in which I've prayed: the cathedral; the huge National Shrine; the twelve altars at Catholic University; the little German church where our family always went to midnight Mass as I grew up; the Trappist monastery, where I'd pray in the dark of early morning; the great chapel at St. Mark's seminary, built on one of the highest hills of the great bowl that surrounds the city of Erie and gradually slopes down into the harbor; the chapel at Paca Street, filled with the voices of the seminarians, singing the Latin Gregorian chant.

A few years ago I made a retreat at Fatima, in Portugal. There Mary came to the little ones. I was deeply moved by the faith of the people of Portugal, who came by the tens of thousands by car, by bus, on foot, by pack animal—not for a festival but for renewal. And to hear a message: the uncomplaining offering of the daily difficulties of ordinary life, and a daily rosary. I took a side trip to Avila and spent a day at the convent of the Incarnation and a morning in the town square, next to the gleaming statue of St. Teresa of Avila. The birds circled around in hundreds, each one lovely, each one important to God. I read some of my breviary there, and I said my rosary, with the prayer Our Lady taught the children: "Oh, my Jesus, forgive us our sins; save us from the fires of hell. Lead all souls to heaven, especially those who are in most need of your mercy."

I decided at Fatima to say fifteen decades of the rosary every day. From Mom and Dad I learned not to be fly-by-night; so I keep that resolution.

Now, in spring and summer and fall at The Lodge, I pray in the rough outdoor chapel. A small building, not much more than ten feet square, made of slab wood and tree trunks split in half for benches, and large screened windows on every side. On whatever bench I sit, I seem to be in the middle of the pine woods. There's one stained glass window, left over from when a large church in Erie was built. The rough chunks of deeply colored glass act like a prism for the sunlight. The sole recognizable symbol, near the top of the window, is the word "Be." Because I like *being*, I suggested to Kevin, who designed the building and supervised the work of it, that we use it, even though it was not as rustic as the rest.

The tabernacle rests in an aged cherry stump cemented into the ground. It's highly polished but still gnarled. Over it hangs a sanctuary lamp, lighted when the Blessed Sacrament is present. At night the candle's light is visible from many parts of the grounds, like the red vigil light my mother always placed in the back window of our house on Christmas Eve—visible out in the fields, to anyone who might be lost.

Kevin is back in prison now. He worked with us for a few years, shook off the remnants of a series of foster families and a long period of imprisonment. Then he went on to a good job, a tremendous income when oil fields were important in Texas, and a revival of drug use that carried him back to prison. I see him sometimes and hear from him. He's trying to help the men who are on death row.

At a Mass in this rough chapel, everything else goes away but an ex-convict or two. Brother Bernard. A mental patient. A man from the streets who used to be religious. A few volunteers. Brother chooses the readers and the hymns. We call to mind that we are sinners. We hear the word of God, and I underline one part of it or another, and we are quiet.

Then in the middle of the woods, and in a quiet that is a shaft to all the suffering of the world—much of it imprinted in the hearts of those present—we offer the butt ends of our lives:

"What I have left I give you."

On the consecrated altar the bread and wine, their lives, my life this week, is consecrated to God. So that we can become holy.

"In sacrifice and sin offerings you had no pleasure, but a body you have fitted to me. Behold, I come to do your will, O God."

And then the bread and wine respond, to be the Body and Blood of Christ. Christ is docile to my words. But the Body of Christ is also made up of people, whose coming is hesitant, provisional, guarded. Only here, in this Eucharist, we share life with Mary, the virgin mother of God, and

Joseph, and the bag lady, and the man who "looks like a murderer." So I collect our lives and offer praise to God—a hymn distilled out of all the events of our lives.

"This is the chalice of my blood, which will be given for you."

And we are made one with Mary at the foot of the cross, and John Paul, and Mother Teresa, and Con and Gert Peterson, and Oscar McGrew, and Rusty and Kevin and all the rest. I memorize moments that I'm fondest of. Jesus said, "As often as you do this, remember me."

This is the moment the Lord wants me to remember, and live.

Then comes communion—the box lunch that we share to give comfort for another stage of the journey home. Together we know communion. Like in a prison broom closet.

After Mass I love to walk by the pond, to see the frogs splash off the sides to avoid whatever is stealthily approaching them, or I go over to talk to the pigs. Late in the day the men may be coming back from the woods with a trailerful of firewood. One or another may be splitting wood. Deftly. Safely. Knowing that he's doing something worth doing. Something simple and true. Something human.

I can't split wood. I can't cook. I can no longer change a tire. But a man puffing when he's splitting wood or smiling when he's drying dishes reminds me of Peter. His fish and his money were gone, but what he had he gave freely. The farmhouse and some of our other houses are heated with wood that will keep Brother and the men who will come warm for the winter.

☙

In the rare times when I'm at the lodge at night, I go alone to the outdoor chapel. Some of the men may be off at an AA meeting; others may have a video or may be writing a letter. My "prayers" for the day may be over. But I go and sit in the dark that is full of silhouette, and the sound of crickets or frogs—I don't really know the difference. The sanctuary lamp is alive. Like it was at Paca Street.

And I am home.

Pine Avenue is gone. My pastorate is gone—except for a grave that waits for me. But I am home. Only a breath away from the vision of God.

Long ago I learned that holiness is not just something between me and God. No longer do I fear that the closeness of people will cost me my inner life. In the years since I left the seminary, I know that much more matters than God-and-my-soul. In sharing the priesthood of Jesus, I know that "the Spirit of the Lord is upon me, because he has anointed me to bring good news to the poor, to proclaim to the captives release." Tonight I can be quiet in God's presence without finding my heart so crowded by God's people that there is no room for him. "The Lord is in His holy temple. Let all the earth keep silent before Him."

I thank God for each new person, that there is room in his heart, in her heart, for me. That I have room. That we have room for God. I ask for loyalty to Christ every day of whatever days remain, and the faith to recognize the signs of his lead and of his love. But that is not enough. I continue to ask for all the prisoners of the world—those behind bars, and those impaled on TVs, those in factories and in rectories—and for a community to heal them, to share life with them. Even that is not enough.

At least fifteen times every day I say, "Lead all souls to heaven, especially those who are in most need of your mercy." That prayer is enough.

More, I could not ask.